INSPIRING
INNOVATION AND
CREATIVITY IN
YOUNG LEARNERS

INSPIRING
INNOVATION AND
CREATIVITY IN
YOUNG LEARNERS

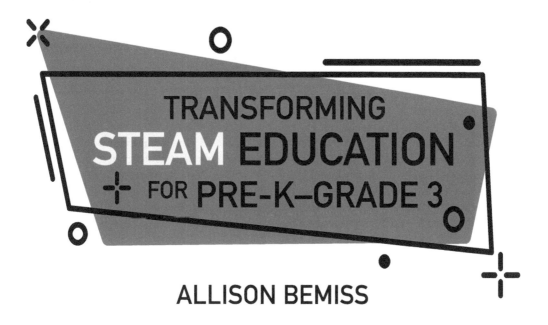

TRANSFORMING
STEAM EDUCATION
FOR PRE-K–GRADE 3

ALLISON BEMISS

PRUFROCK PRESS INC.
WACO, TEXAS

Prufrock Press Inc.
P.O. Box 8813
Waco, TX 76714-8813
Phone: (800) 998-2208
Fax: (800) 240-0333
http://www.prufrock.com

TABLE OF CONTENTS

ACKNOWLEDGMENTS

Alone we can do so little; together we can do so much.

—Helen Keller

Without the help of the educators listed below, this book and its engaging lessons would not have been possible. Thank you for your willingness to pilot these STEAM explorations with your young learners, either by testing the lessons out yourself or allowing me to come in and coteach with you. The opportunity to see the excitement and engagement in the classroom either firsthand, through photographs, or by listening to your stories was so inspiring. It also helped me shape these lessons into more meaningful learning experiences for the little learners and educators that will try them in the future.

- Preschool: Maggie Murphy and Haley Penden, Gamelia Elementary; Cindy Emberton, Joe Harrison Carter Elementary; Amanda Rich, Amy Hammer, and Charity Stoops, Tompkinsville Elementary (Monroe County Public Schools)
- Kindergarten: Tracy Tharp, Hodgenville Elementary (LaRue County Public Schools)
- First Grade: Jessica Riedel, Briarwood Elementary (Warren County Public Schools)
- Second Grade: Renee Johnson, Briarwood Elementary (Warren County Public Schools)
- Third Grade: Nicole Lee, Parker-Bennett-Curry Elementary (Bowling Green Independent Schools)

I'd also like to extend a heartfelt thank you to my amazing team of early childhood (Pre-K–grade 3) enthusiasts whom I have the opportunity to brainstorm with each day. Jamie, Kathy, and Melanie, thank you for packing your bags with every tinkering supply imaginable and helping to test these hands-on, minds-on STEAM explorations across our little corner of the world.

INTRODUCTION

Creativity is the key to innovation. It is up to you to use it as a tool.

—Easton LaChappelle, Founder of Unlimited Tomorrow

What Are Innovation and Creativity?

Thomas Edison didn't invent the light bulb—he *innovated* it. By improving on the function of the light bulb and using different materials to create it, he made it more affordable. Easton LaChappelle didn't invent the robotic arm—he used 3-D printing to reduce the cost by tens of thousands of dollars, making it more affordable and more accessible to those in need. Innovation is the ability to see something in a new or different way. It is the ability to take an idea and adapt it in a way that solves a problem, making it more useful for someone or something in need. Creativity is the tool that drives the idea, making the impossible possible. Creativity and innovation are so closely intertwined that, in school, we shouldn't think of them as totally separate areas. When we strengthen our students' abilities to think outside of the box or outside of their current frame of reference with creative learning opportunities, we also strengthen their ability to innovate. LaChappelle was only 14 when he created his first robotic arm from LEGO bricks.

Exploring with LEGO bricks, building with blocks, investigating why paint changes colors when it's mixed, journaling about topics of concern, sharing ideas with friends, dressing in a lab coat, and inspecting items collected outside with a microscope—these creative play-based learning opportunities are the foundation from which innovative thinking is built. These experiences are critical in early childhood (ages 3–8) because they become the schema that young learners will connect to as they explore content throughout the rest of their lives.

How to Encourage Little Learners to Share Big Ideas

There are many helpful models of innovation and critical thinking both in the business world and in the educational setting. The four that inspired the ideas for the innovation strategies in this book are Bloom's (1956) taxonomy, the Innovation Model (Project GEMS, 2011), design thinking (Stanford d.school, n.d.), and Sheffield's (2003) heuristic for creative and innovative mathematicians. The strategies in this book were also influenced by the ideas and beliefs found in *Mindsets in the Classroom* (Ricci, 2017), *Strategies That Work* (Harvey & Goudvis, 2007), and *Creating Innovators* (Wagner, 2012).

Strategies for Innovation and Creativity

If we want to transform STEAM (science, technology, engineering, arts, and mathematics) education for our youngest learners, we must expect them to think critically and creatively by learning to use and own the following strategies:

- making connections (schema),
- growth mindset (learning from mistakes),
- empathy (understanding the problems of others),
- wonder (questioning),
- inference (noticing, connecting to schema, and reasoning), and
- reflection (thinking metacognitively about exploring and learning).

Chapters 2–7 of this book feature additional information on these strategies, as well as a STEAM investigation that models each strategy. Note that you would rarely, if ever, use a strategy in a STEAM exploration in isolation. Rich learning experiences often are interdisciplinary, meaning they will stretch across content areas. The same notion is true with innovative thinking routines. A rich lesson will organically use more than one strategy. That said, it is a good idea to explicitly teach one strategy at a time to young learners. Students are likely using strategies as they problem solve that they don't yet have the language to describe; they may be able to tell you what the exploration reminds them of but may not understand that they are making connections.

A Note From a District Administrator

Carlena Sheeran is a district administrator who has successfully implemented STEAM curriculum and rigorous learning experiences in the classrooms in her schools. Ms. Sheeran builds community and buy-in from families and other educators by celebrating these students' and teachers' accomplishments on various social media platforms. She shared some advice on how she approaches the adoption and implementation of these types of initiatives:

We are extremely thoughtful and thorough when we purchase materials/resources for our preschool program. Because time is a precious thing, we are very specific in our plan for using our resources. With our implementation of *Hands-On STEAM Explorations for Young Learners* [Bemiss, 2018], we were intentional in the time frame for our teachers to teach the lessons to our students (one per month). I try to keep the reflections from teachers as simple as sending me post-photos from these fabulous lessons.

—Carlena Sheeran, Director of Early Childhood, Hardin County Public Schools

Readiness to Think at High Levels

Before students can be expected to explore and achieve at high levels, it is important to think about Maslow's (1943) hierarchy of needs and how it relates to each of your young learners. Students must feel safe and secure and have all of their foundational needs met before they should be expected to move to the higher levels of Bloom's (1956) taxonomy. As an educator, you are responsible for teaching the whole child, as he or she comes to you, not just the content of the lesson. Chapter 1 shares more information about establishing a learning environment that meets the unique needs of your students.

A Note From an English Language Learner Teacher

When considering how to engage English learners in these [STEAM] activities, think about providing multiple entry points into the activity based on their proficiency levels. This type of scaffolding can be accomplished through visuals, videos, models, realia, cooperative learning activities, translation, tasks designed to support language, blended learning, immediate feedback, and student choice.
—LoriAnn Martin, District EL (English Language) Consultant, Warren County Public Schools

Personalized Learning

Each student who walks into your classroom comes with his or her own set of schema, challenges, and strengths. The beauty of open-ended STEAM explorations, like those featured in this book, is that there is no ceiling. Students can take learning to their own level of readiness. Whether a child is precocious, is an English language learner, has a motor impairment or a speech delay, or is a twice-exceptional learner whose needs are a combination of these, STEAM education is for him or her. Innovative thinking and minds-on, hands-on thinking opportunities are for *all* learners. As Roberts and Inman (2015) discussed in their book *Strategies for Differentiating Instruction*, there is no such thing as a "one-size-fits-all" lesson or classroom for students. There is a need to adapt content for each student, which makes STEAM explorations the perfect tool for differentiating instruction organically. The innovative and creative thinking strategies shared in this book are open-ended. The investigations require young learners to share their wonderings and test the questions. Investigations are based on student interests and use materials of each student's choice. This allows each student's individual strengths and areas of growth to be addressed in each exploration.

A Note From a Principal

Each and every student deserves the same opportunities as their peers. A label (such as SPED, EL, etc.) is nothing more than that . . . a label. Each child CAN be taught with rigor. It may look a little different based on a child's academic needs, but all students (no matter their ability) deserve the opportunity to question, to infer, and to make connections. We should never underestimate what a child can do. They will always prove us wrong. An administrator needs to be the one delivering this philosophy to his staff. This philosophy should be evident beyond spoken words by his daily approach to educating a child. Don't be afraid to walk that walk!

—Wes Cottongim, Principal, Cumberland Trace Elementary School

Make Learning Relatable to the Age and Interests of the Student

In early childhood (up to age 8), we are laying the foundation for the rest of a student's educational career. When students have positive attitudes and beliefs about STEAM experiences as young learners, they are more likely to feel successful in those content areas. As students get older, if they feel successful in STEAM content areas, they will be more likely to take advanced coursework in middle and high school. In turn, this puts students on a path to explore interests in STEAM careers. Does this mean that every child will choose to be an engineer? No, of course not. However, the thinking strategies used in STEAM investigations are skills that all children need for lifelong learning in any discipline.

A Note From an Early Childhood Consultant

STEAM-rich environments serve as catalysts for critical thinking, exploration, and communication for young children. Young children are naturally inquisitive and become academic risk takers when given the opportunity to participate in open-ended, high-level learning activities. STEAM activities provide a venue for trial and error, and help create a foundation for critical thinking for lifelong learning.

—Beth Schaeffer, Preschool Consultant,
Warren County Public Schools

The ability to think critically and creatively is advantageous for every student in your class. How do you make this skill relatable for young learners? First, choose STEAM challenges that pique your students' curiosity and are relatable to their lives. Second, create an environment that is engaging. For example, if students are working in a chemistry lab, make sure they have lab and safety equipment, not only for safety and function, but also to help them feel that they belong in a lab. When a child dresses up as a lion, she becomes a lion. When a child dresses up as a scientist, he becomes a scientist. The vocabulary that young learners use, the materials they interact with, and the confidence they exhibit will match the environment created for them. Third, expect big things from your little learners. Share rigorous vocabulary that matches topics of study, expect students to share ideas, and be respectful of their thoughts.

A Note From a District Gifted and Talented Teacher and Coordinator

Young children are avid investigators—innately curious, full of wonder, and eager to explore and invent. Open-ended STEAM explorations are fully inclusive as they allow students to make authentic connections at their own pace and in their own way. No child is labeled as being "behind" or "ahead" in meeting a rigidly-defined outcome, nor told they have reached an understanding the "wrong" way. Instead, each student's wonderings and observations are honored and allowed to guide his/her naturally-unfolding and inherently differentiated learning experience.

—Jennifer Sheffield, District Gifted and Talented Consultant and EDGE Academy Lead Teacher, Simpson County Public Schools

Play, Explore, and Innovate Together

Possibly the most important point in this book is to play, explore, and innovate together with your students. If students see you thinking aloud as you struggle to solve a problem, if they hear you talking about an issue you care about, if they hear you wondering, and if they see you smiling as you explore, they will learn by observing you. They will learn that STEAM is exciting from your smiles. They will learn that it is hard work when they see you persevere through a challenge. They will learn that making mistakes doesn't mean that you're not smart.

Our students are always watching our behaviors. If we approach STEAM, innovation, and creative thinking with confidence, perseverance, and excitement, our students will do the same. This is also true for families. By hosting family STEAM events or sending home STEAM backpacks (see p. 23), families can play and explore together. Any of the explorations in the book can be modified for use in a family event or as a take-home activity. There is nothing more powerful for a young learner than to see the adults he or she cares for engaged and excited as they explore STEAM concepts.

Innovation and Creativity Tools

This guide features the following tools to inspire innovation and foster creativity:

- tips on how to develop an emotional and physical environment that supports critical and creative thinking;
- tips for family engagement and communication (e.g., see *Seasonal STEAM Bucket Lists* and *10 Things to Ask Instead of "What Did You Learn?"* included in the color insert of this book and at https://www.prufrock.com/Inspiring-Innovation-and-Creativity-in-Young-Learners-Resources.aspx);
- a brief introduction of each topic for innovation;
- a minds-on, hands-on STEAM investigation for each innovation topic;
- innovation student journal pages that can be used as preassessments, reflection, brainstorming, or classroom anchor charts; and
- standards connections for STEAM explorations.

A Note From a Principal

The fact is, life doesn't present itself in a cookie-cutter form. Our job as educators goes far beyond paper/pencil tasks. We as educators have to present opportunities for students that allow them to think outside the box to solve problems. We are doing our students a disservice if we don't allow them to think abstractly and to explore possibilities. We must present opportunities for students to wonder, to infer, and to question. This prepares them for more than our curriculum's content; it prepares them for life's unpredictability. We (educators and students) must be able to facilitate opportunities for our kids to investigate!

—Wes Cottongim, Principal, Cumberland Trace Elementary

CHAPTER 1

AN ENVIRONMENT FOR **INNOVATION** AND **CREATIVITY**

There are few things in an innovative and creative classroom that are more important than the environment in which learning occurs. The space for learning will set the stage to either inspire innovation or stifle creativity. In education, *environment* is a loaded word because it encompasses so much. This chapter will take a look at both the physical environment and the emotional environment of the classroom. The chapter will also explore important topics and describe how to do the following:

- implement creative approaches to administering preassessment to determine interests and readiness levels,
- talk with children to encourage thinking,
- design a meaningful (and sometimes magical) environment, and
- encourage ownership in the classroom.

Physical Environment

You may have a classroom with a ton of space, or you may be teaching in a repurposed closet (speaking from experience). Whatever your space, large or small, you can make it work for your students.

When designing the physical space, keep the following three ideas in mind.

Kids' Level, Not Adults' Level

All of the artwork, anchor charts, and materials—everything you can think of that is designed for the learners in your classroom—should be at their eye level. This is their space, and you want to be sure they have access to it.

Organization

Think about the grouping patterns you will use for students throughout the year. Likely, they will have times in their day when they are working independently, in small groups or pairs, or with the whole group. You want to be sure you have designated space for each of these patterns. Be creative with the seating options; desks and chairs are not the only options. There are many alternative seating options that work well for young learners. Figure 1 shares how teachers Stacy Garden (grades 2–3) and Renee Johnson (grade 2) have implemented alternative seating in their classroom environments.

If you are working with limited space, consider using beach towels, yoga mats, or rolled-up bath mats stored in a basket for moveable small-group or independent work areas. These mats can also be taken outside if you choose to do an outdoor lesson.

Also, think about the needs of the students in your classroom. Do you have a space in your room for them to find books? Do you have spaces in your room for them to explore writing, science, or math? Designated spaces with materials that support topics of interest are so important to encourage innovation. If you don't have enough room to incorporate all of these areas, consider using suitcases to make portable exploration areas. The portable suitcase stations can be taken outside to encourage learning outdoors. For example, the portable innovation station pictured in Figure 2 includes two "flying toys" (see the STEAM exploration in Chapter 5), a pencil, and a student journal.

Another idea (from Alisha Sharp, a Head Start Teacher at Joe Harrison Carter Elementary, Monroe County, KY) is to keep all of your Makerspace materials in a rolling drawer system with task cards, pictured in Figure 3. This way you can pull the Makerspace in and out when children need access to these items. With a little creativity, any space can be transformed into an innovative learning environment.

Materials

Young learners need "things" in order to learn, explore, and share. They need access to magnifying glasses to take a look at the leaf they found on the playground, or paper and a clipboard to sketch that butterfly they want to tell you about. You want to be sure they have access to these commonly used items.

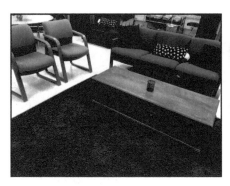

Figure 1. Alternative seating options.

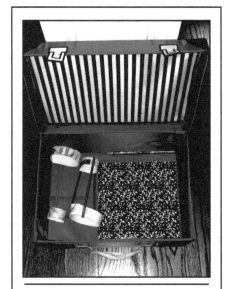

Figure 2. Portable suitcase.

Figure 3. STEAM Makerspace cart.

Keeping the materials students often need—like clipboards, paper, pencils, scissors, glue, magnifying glasses, and safety goggles—in a place that students can access when they are investigating promotes independence. These items should be located in a container that is clearly labeled with words as well as photos for developing readers. Keeping materials organized in clearly defined and labeled spaces lets students know not only where to get materials, but also how to clean up after themselves.

> ## A Note From an Occupational Therapist
>
> Hands-on learning not only facilitates motor skill development, but also enhances executive functioning skills, such as planning, sequencing, and problem solving.
> —Nicole Martin, Occupational Therapist, Warren County Public Schools

Lab safety and investigation guidelines are also critical components of the classroom environment. You want to make safety as clear and easy to understand as possible for young learners. Post the following guidelines in the classroom and review them prior to each lesson to help students play and explore safely (Bemiss, 2018):

L: Learn by exploring!
(*Trying and failing is learning; failing to try is not.*)
A: Always keep materials *away* from your eyes, nose, mouth, and hands.
(*As needed, wear safety goggles and gloves to keep your body safe.*)
B: Be aware.
(*Notice what's happening around you.*) (p. 2)

> ## A Note From an Early Childhood Coach
>
> When the physical learning environment is filled with a variety of learning tools and open-ended materials, the young child's mind is activated with an intuitive curiosity for wondering and inferencing.
> —Jamie Spugnardi, Director of Instructional Services, Green River Regional Educational Cooperative

Emotional Environment

If the physical environment is what students see, then the emotional environment is what students feel. The emotional environment is extremely important in the innovative and creative classroom. Innovation in its simplest form means trying new ideas that haven't yet been tested. Anytime students are trying something new, failure, mistakes, and vulnerability should be expected. Ed Catmull, a computer scientist and president of Pixar Animation Studios and Walt Disney Animation Studios, discussed the importance of candor (i.e., open, honest, and frank discussions) in the creative process in *Creativity, Inc.* (Catmull & Wallace, 2014). If our goal is creative and innovative thinking, then it makes sense that we can learn from our students about how to best engage and challenge them to move forward as creative thinkers. We want to ensure that our students have these opportunities as they explore and learn together. Mistakes, failure, candor—these experiences aren't easy for adults, and they certainly aren't easy for children. In order to develop critical and creative thinking, children must know that they work in an environment that is safe—both physically and emotionally.

Maslow's (1943) hierarchy of needs is a great place to look when thinking about what children need in their emotional environment. They need to feel safe, a sense of belonging, and a sense of accomplishment in order to reach their full potential.

A Note From a First-Grade Teacher

In this photo, students were asked to dissect a seed in groups of two. One student pictured has Cerebral palsy and has limited mobility on his right side. His partner allowed him to do hand-over-hand so he could participate in the activity in its entirety. Creating a community where students feel safe and trust their teachers and peers is imperative for academic success. From day one, it is important to focus and celebrate abilities of every student. Your students will begin to do the same and believe not only in themselves, but in their peers as well. They will strive to help one another when they see the opportunity. Everyone wins, and learning happens in so many incredible ways.

—Jessica Riedel, First-Grade Teacher, Briarwood Elementary, Warren County Public Schools

Ritual and Ceremonies

A classroom should feel like a family. A dear friend and mentor of mine, Nancy Huston, taught me early in my career that without a family atmosphere in my class, classroom management would be a struggle and many students wouldn't feel comfortable sharing ideas. In *Life in a Crowded Place*, Peterson (1992) discussed how families celebrate birthdays, accomplishments, and holidays. Each family has its own norms and experiences that make it unique. You can bring these ideas to the classroom.

Bead ceremony. In my classroom, we enjoyed a bead ceremony at the beginning and ending of each year. We sat in a circle, and each threaded a bead onto a necklace, discussing how each person's bead was unique just like we were all unique. As children threaded the necklace, they would share a wish or goal for the year. We hung this necklace on the board where it was visible throughout the entire year, and we reflected on it. When one student moved out of our class, she looked at me with tears and asked if I was going to take away her bead. We had an emergency family meeting (see p. 17) to discuss this situation. Of course, the students all decided that there was no way we could take away this student's bead; once you were in the classroom family, you were always in the family. One child suggested that we make wishes for the student's new school on a new necklace, and just like that, a new classroom ritual was born. This student had her wish necklace to wear on the first day at her new school.

Singing/mottos/chants. In our class we sang—a lot. Singing builds phonological awareness and introduces concepts like rhyming, beat, rhythm, and poetry. It is also a great transition activity. Filling space or clean-up time with this literacy activity brings joy to the classroom. However, one of the best things about this oral language activity is that it builds community, especially if you include some silly or unique song that other classes aren't often singing. A former student of mine, now in college, recently mentioned that he could still remember our class circled together singing "Country Roads" by John Denver; years later, he could vividly remember our classroom environment.

A Note From a Former Young Learner

The songs, family meetings, and being read to weren't science and math lessons—they were simply fun. In making school an enjoyable place to be, those activities made me excited to learn and be part of the classroom. I think because I was excited to be part of my classroom community, it made learning easier and more meaningful.
—Reed Mattison, Student, Western Kentucky University

For the youngest learners, Bailey (2000) shared many wonderful rituals that can be done quickly to establish connection and community in the book *I Love You Rituals*. These rituals are also great to share with parents at family events.

Celebrate. Families celebrate everything—whether it's a birthday, a new job, or a lost tooth. Classroom families should do the same. Like rituals, celebrations offer an opportunity for children to get to know one another and build trust.

Family meetings. Family meetings are a time for students (and the teacher) to share concerns and voice accomplishments. The family meeting agenda should be limited to 3–5 items each week; beyond that, discussing the items can become unmanageable. Items on the agenda can include issues a student or group of students is facing that need to be problem solved. Note that bullying is not an item for a family meeting—that should be dealt with immediately. However, not taking turns on the swing at the playground would be a perfect family meeting item.

As children mention their concerns, you can model thinking aloud and problem solving. Saying things like "I understand your frustration with . . ." will not only help solve the problem at hand, but also model appropriate language for children to use when they are working through hard conversations during STEAM investigations. The agenda for the family meeting should also include a page for listing celebrations. On this sheet, children can add anything they would like to share as a celebration recognizing their own or a friend's accomplishment. Accomplishments might include placing first at a recent gymnastic meet or noticing that a friend finished his first chapter book. Family meetings offer a perfect time for celebrating and problem solving.

Kindness matters. Kindness chains (as seen in Figure 4) are another great way for students to share acts of kindness for others. Ask students to notice kindness from others in the class or around the school, and then either write or draw what they noticed on a strip of paper. These strips can then be linked to create a kindness chain as a visual reminder for acts of kindness. Conscious Discipline (2019) recommended using kindness flowers as a part of a kindness ritual with young students. Bouquets can serve as visual symbols for acts of kindness, as seen in Figure 5. Either of these are wonderful options to build community and trust in the classroom environment.

Mindfulness

Growth mindset is an important term in education; it's even the basis for Chapter 3 in this book. However, we cannot expect young learners to understand how to immediately deal with the frustration of failure without teaching them mindfulness strategies to redirect their mindset. The following are helpful resources on mindfulness specifically geared toward young children:

- *Breathe Like a Bear* by Kira Willey: This picture book shares 30 age-appropriate mindful moment activities for children.
- S.T.A.R. Breathing Tool by Conscious Discipline (https://consciousdiscipline.com/videos/s-t-a-r-breathing-tool): S.T.A.R. stands for Smile, Take

Figure 4. Kindness chains from Drakes Creek Middle School.

Figure 5. Kindness bouquet from Ms. Judy Ged's Pre-K class.

a deep breath, And Relax. Using these strategies alongside growth mindset best practices will be better prepare your students to see mistakes as the start to learning.

- Turtle Breathing (Take 5): For this exercise, children use their hands as a model to facilitate deep breathing. Have students breathe in as they slowly trace a finger up their thumb, and then exhale slowly as they trace their finger down their thumb. Students will continue this pattern until they have completed all five fingers (see Figure 6).

Creating experiences such as the ones listed in this section lays the foundation for building a community of learners and establishes trust. If children are expected to make mistakes, learn from failure, and receive honest and frank feedback, the classroom should have both community and trust.

Make Learning Meaningful (and Magical)

Young learners need to see themselves as the innovators they are. It is our job as their teachers to do whatever we can to make them feel that way. A few ideas include the following.

Figure 6. Turtle breathing (take 5) mindfulness strategy.

Make Lab Coats

Along with protecting students' clothing, lab coats go a long way to making children feel like innovators, engineers, scientists, or artists. Lab coats can be easily made by cutting oversized T-shirts up the middle (see Figure 7).

Decorate Your Classroom

When we are celebrating something at home, what do we do? We decorate! The same is true in your classroom. Setting the environment for learning can engage kids from the moment they walk in the door. If you are doing an investigation with a space theme, like the first and last explorations in this book (see Chapters 2 and 7), you might turn down the lights, hang stars, and put up twinkle lights. You might cover the door in mylar blankets or foil, so it looks like a space station. Why is this important? When STEAM is engaging and relatable to the age and interest of students, they are more likely to see the learning as en

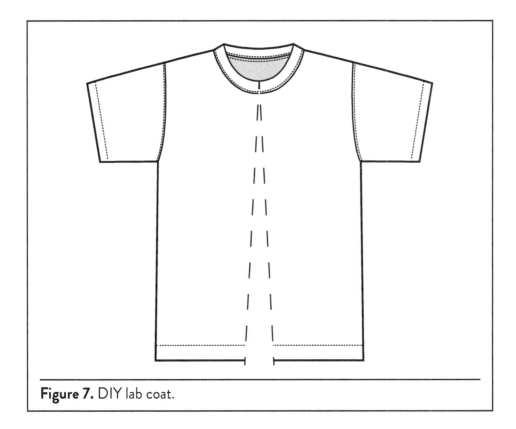

Figure 7. DIY lab coat.

joyable. They also begin to see how they fit into this area of study. Something as simple as making your door look like a spaceship hatch or hanging some twinkle lights to look like stars can help your students step out of their current frame and begin to feel like rocket scientists.

Change Up the Classroom

The classroom should be ever changing based on learners' interests and topics of study. If you are studying space, you want to be sure that your book nook (or mobile learning station) has books and other items to encourage curiosity. Consider putting a rocket or a tent decorated to look like a space station in the book nook. If you have centers in your classroom, it's a good idea to change those regularly. Figure 8 shows how RuthAnn Smith, a preschool teacher at Rineyville Elementary in Hardin County, transformed her dramatic play center into an airplane. When you change materials or centers, you change the vocabulary that students are accessing. The vocabulary used in an airport is very different than the vocabulary used in a housekeeping area. Another clever idea to promote engagement and student ownership is to let children help you determine the materials that will be available to them. These are called Book Tastings or Tinker and Think Tastings.

Figure 8. Airplane center.

Book Tastings

Book Tastings are modeled after food tastings. Students sample texts by scanning words and looking at the pictures or photographs to decide what they might enjoy. Some teachers put out tablecloths or offer a snack while children do this activity. The steps for creating and conducting a Book Tasting are as follows:

1. Gather books on topics of interest.
2. Ask students to scan the books, looking at photos and reading titles or other words that grab their interests. (This activity provides a perfect opportunity for young children to learn what it means to "scan" a book.)
3. After learners look through the books, have them partner share which books they would like to read in the book nook or during independent reading time.
4. Make sure these books are available to read in the book nook or other appropriate stations in the room.

Booklist

Books that feature inspiring innovators include:
- *Girls Think of Everything: Stories of Ingenious Inventions by Women* by Catherine Thimmesh
- *Inventors Who Changed the World* (Little Heroes Book 2) by Heidi Poelman
- *Kid Scientists: True Tales of Childhood From Science Superstars* by David Stabler
- *Never Too Young!: 50 Unstoppable Kids Who Made a Difference* by Aileen Weintraub
- *This Little Scientist: A Discovery Primer* by Joan Holub

Book Tastings, continued

Books that feature innovative and creative thinking include:
- *Beautiful Oops!* by Barney Saltzberg
- *The Dot* by Peter H. Reynolds
- *The Invisible Boy* by Trudy Ludwig
- *Ish* by Peter H. Reynolds
- *The Most Magnificent Thing* by Ashley Spires
- *The OK Book* by Amy Krouse Rosenthal
- *The Wonderful Things You Will Be* by Emily Winfield Martin

Tinker and Think Tastings

An interesting twist on Book Tastings are Tinker and Think Tastings. Follow the same procedure as you would for a Book Tasting, but, in addition to the books, add in the manipulatives you will be using for upcoming lessons, such as pattern blocks or STEAM toys that you would like to include in a lesson or science center (e.g., a kid-friendly microscope with a bag of items to view or a coding game). Explain to students that they are just sampling these activities to determine what they'd most like to spend their time on later. This activity gives young learners the opportunity to participate in literacy skills using a mixture of literature and hands-on materials. Tinker and Think Tastings offer children an opportunity to think critically and own their environment. See Figure 9 for an example of a Tinker and Think Tasting.

Materials List

- **Reading:** books, photos, and articles on innovators, innovation, or topics of study
- **Toys:** robotics toys, logic puzzles, coding games, prisms, tangrams, pattern blocks
- **Tools:** measurement tools, microscopes, magnifying glasses, horseshoe magnets

Figure 9. Tinker and Think Tasting.

Family Partners

Your students spend a lot of time with you at school, but they also spend a lot of time away from you. Sharing ideas with families about ways to explore together can help build not only mathematics and science skills, but also literacy. The resource pages located in the insert of this book can be shared with families. The STEAM bucket lists are a great way to share ideas for family STEAM explorations. On that same note, it's also sometimes difficult to get students to communicate their learning both at school and at home. The resource page *10 Things to Ask Instead of "What Did You Learn?"* would be helpful to share with families to encourage communication and family engagement.

Another engaging idea is to send home STEAM backpacks with young learners for families to explore together. For example, each backpack could include a magnifying glass, a journal, and instructions for the family to take a nature walk together in their yard or a nearby park. These backpacks could also include books that celebrate innovators in all content areas along with accompanying tasks. The STEAM exploration shared in Chapter 5 would make a wonderful backpack activity for families. You could send home a copy of the book *The Girl Who Thought in Pictures*, along with straws and cut cardstock (as described in the lesson). Families could then enjoy reading the book and making their own paper flyers together. The sky is the limit with STEAM backpacks, but they are wonderful tools to engage families in minds-on, hands-on experiences together.

A Note From an Early Childhood Consultant

Family STEAM events are a great way for educators to partner with families on ways to use everyday learning opportunities. By empowering [families] to use activities that enhance problem-solving skills as well as creative thinking, it allows us to extend learning beyond the walls of the classroom. By providing "out of the box" opportunities, we are able to foster high-need skills, such as science, technology, pre-engineering, and design, in a developmentally appropriate way.

—Krista Graves, Early Childhood Consultant, Bowling Green Independent Schools

Readiness and Interests

One of the most important things you can do to make learning meaningful is to know what your kids know and how they want to know it. Alongside traditional preassessments that your school or district may facilitate for your students, informal preassessments and inventories are a good way to learn specific information about what children know. The Draw A Scientist test was developed in 1983 to determine students' stereotypes and understanding of what a scientist was and who could be a scientist (Yong, 2018). The resource pages shared at the end of this chapter, *Draw an Innovator* and *Diagram of an Innovator*, are based on the Draw a Scientist test but offer children the opportunity to think about more than just scientists.

When using these pages, you may want to discuss what the word *innovator* means (i.e., someone who creates or shares new ideas or a changes current products or popular ideas). You can give examples of innovators, but I'd encourage you to avoid giving a lot of explanation or direction for these activities in advance. Because this is preassessment, you don't want to influence students' drawings. For young students, starting with the simple *Draw an Innovator* page would be most appropriate. When working with older children who understand how text features are used to communicate and organize ideas, you may consider using *Diagram of an Innovator*. On this page, you would simply ask students to draw a diagram of an innovator listing important characteristics in the blanks (e.g., "a mouth that shares new ideas or gives feedback," "hands that build and create," "a mind that looks for problems or thinks of a way to solve problems"). After I shared this idea with a group of teachers at the Kentucky Association for the Gifted Conference, a teacher at Kentucky's School for the Blind suggested also giving students the option to *Build an Innovator* using common classroom materials, like pipe cleaners, glue, and construction paper—basically any material you have readily available in your classroom. Changing the verb from *draw* to *build* not only encourages a hands-on approach, but also is a good alternative for students with visual impairment. All three options, *Draw an Innovator, Diagram of an Innovator,* and *Build an Innovator,* are included in this text. Regardless of which option you determine is more appropriate for the children you serve, the information gained through this activity is important in helping you to assess students' current level of readiness in their understanding of innovation and innovators.

These resource pages can be used as pre- and postassessments. As your learners complete more and more of the STEAM challenges in this book, they will begin to learn the strategies of innovation (like learning from mistakes), and you will see that learning reflected in their *Draw an Innovator* drawings. You will also notice that your students' drawings of innovators look less stereotypical and more like the students. Several other journal pages throughout this book could also be used as preassessments to learn about the readiness levels or interests of your students. For example, *Everything I Want to Know About* and *How I Want To Learn About* in Chapter 2 can help you learn about topics that interest students in a particular unit of study. As you look through the student journal pages, think about how they may be used before, during, and after instruction to facilitate continuous progress and learning.

Organized Chaos

Once a teacher described my classroom as "organized chaos" after watching my students engaged in a minds-on, hands-on investigation. Although at first I was unsure how I felt about this description, once I'd pondered the idea, I decided that was exactly the type of environment I strived to create for my young learners. It's chaotic because learning is personalized. Students may be working independently or in small groups depending on the task and student choice. They may be using slightly different materials to investigate their unique wondering question developed around a central topic of study. This can look like chaos at first glance. However, a closer look will reveal organization. Materials should be clearly labeled and organized for students. Cleanup and safety equipment should be out and in use. Anchor charts, diagrams, or vocabulary should be posted for student reference as they explore. As unpredictable as the STEAM environment is, the children's interactions should also be somewhat predictable.

The following list shares some "look for" questions to help teachers determine if students are engaged.

- **Movement:** Are students busy planning, collecting materials, creating, or testing?
- **Excitement:** Are students feeling emotion (smiling, frowning, puzzling)? Did the voice level in your classroom go up a bit?
- **Candor:** Are students engaging in honest and open conversation using thinking strategies?
- **Moving forward:** Are students progressing through the stages of exploration (i.e., thinking, planning, creating, testing, redesigning)?

If your answer is "yes" to these questions, then you know that your students are participating in successful organized chaos. If the answer is "no," then you know that students need some prompting, guidance, or modeling from you. Remember, it is always better to ask students a question when they are pondering than to give them an answer. After all, the purpose of these explorations is to teach them that they are young innovators. Productive struggle, messes, excitement, and cleanup are all a part of being an innovator.

Classroom environment is the key to any successful innovative and creative thinking experience. We often spend all of our time thinking about the content, thinking strategies, or materials needed for lessons, but the classroom environment is the foundation for all learning that will occur. This environment is established well before the children enter the room, but it should be changed and should reflect the unique experiences, needs, and interests of the changing young learners in your classroom.

Resource Pages:
Innovation

The following resource pages can be used as pre- and postassessments as your students learn more about innovators.

- Draw an Innovator
- Diagram of an Innovator
- Build an Innovator

Draw an Innovator

Diagram of an Innovator

1 _____

4 _____

2 _____

5 _____

3 _____

Build an Innovator

CHAPTER 2
POWERFUL CONNECTIONS

Schema, or a child's current understanding and the ability to connect and adapt his or her knowledge, is the foundation from which all learning is built. Here's a simple explanation of how it works. A young child might have a cat at home. She calls that animal "cat." Later she sees a dog at a neighbor's house. She sees a furry animal with four legs, and she shouts, "cat!" Her grandmother may point out that the animal is a dog, explaining that dogs are larger or that they bark. The child learns a new word, *dog*, based off of her current understanding, or schema, of a cat. Once the child is in school, new learning is created in exactly the same way—it must be connected to things that she already understands.

How Do Teachers Help Create Powerful Connections?

Innovation and creative thinking are always connected to a person's schema. Brick by brick, book by book, dirt by craft stick, we must help lay this foundation for our young learners. It is one of our most important jobs as early childhood educators. Early in my teaching career, the book *Strategies That Work* (Harvey & Goudvis, 2007) changed my literacy instruction. One of the first strategies from the book that I tried with my students was using sticky notes to have children identify the three types of connections as they read or interacted with media.

- T-S: Text to Self—A child connects what is read to his own experience.
- T-T: Text to Text—A child connects what is read to something he has read before.
- T-W: Text to World—A child connects what is read to something happening in the world.

As I implemented this strategy in my reading classes, I quickly realized that these connections were applicable in more subjects than reading, which makes sense because literacy experiences occur in every facet of the day. I began to ask students, "What do you notice, and what does this remind you of?" For young children, I would provide the sentence starter, "This reminds me of . . ." Posing open-ended questions and using these kinds of sentence starters allow teachers to have a better understanding of what a child has already experienced regarding a particular topic. These questions are actually an informal preassessment to help teachers plan instruction and learn more about a student's prior knowledge and interests.

When working with young learners, or learners who may not have had opportunities to build schema in a particular topic, your most valuable role then becomes to provide those experiences for that child. When planning a unit of study, ask yourself, "How can I build schema to help this student make connections to what we are investigating?" The following are a few ideas of things you can do to encourage powerful connections in innovative and creative thinking.

- Model T-S, T-T, and T-W connections and provide opportunities for students to share these connections. This will help students relate to important ideas and schema they need to comprehend and work through problems during the STEAM investigation.
- Understand that your young learners are still actively developing schema to connect. Creating experiences to help build background knowledge and connections to STEAM investigations is critical in innovative thinking and problem solving.
- Teach children thinking stems (e.g., This reminds me of . . .) that can help them communicate connections and recognize when schema are helping them to solve a problem.
- Plan for various ways to build schema ties into Universal Design for Learning (UDL). UDL's three principles require multiple representations of content presented, multiple types of expression or sharing information, and multiple means of engagement (CAST, 2018). If teachers receive students' input on the innovation student journal page *How I Want to Learn About*, this informal preassessment will help guide the UDL process as the teacher plans for multiple types of representation, expression, and engagement. More information about UDL can be found at http://udlguidelines.cast.org.

Journaling and Anchor Charts: Connections

The following can be used as anchor charts or journal pages for students to record thinking as they explore this strategy and learn to make powerful connections.

- *Everything I Know About*: This journal page requires students to jot down or draw everything they know about a particular topic of study. (This page is used in the model STEAM exploration featured in this chapter.)
- *Everything I Want To Know About*: In this variation of the preceding organizer, students are asked to share everything they want to know about a topic. This is helpful when students may have limited prior knowledge about a topic. This tool also works as an innovative preassessment.
- *I Noticed, This Reminds Me of*: Students will write or draw something they noticed while observing, reading, or listening, and then share what this observation reminds them of.
- *Notice and Know Chart*: In this variation of the preceding tool, students will also share what they noticed; however, this time they will share something they know about that observation. This variation is also useful for older learners because it is organized as a chart, allowing student to share multiple observations.
- *How I Learned About*: On this journal page, students will draw or write to describe how they learned about a particular topic of study. This page can be completed as a reflection at the end of a lesson or before an investigation to help students connect to prior experiences.
- *How I Want to Learn About*: In this variation of the preceding tool, students will describe how they want to learn about a particular topic of study. This question allows students to share with you the modalities in which they prefer to learn. If you are implementing a UDL learning experience, this page would help you better understand what types of multiple representations you may want to plan for an upcoming lesson or unit of study.

Everything I Know About . . .

Write topic name.

Everything I Want to Know About . . .

_____

Write topic name.

I Noticed . . .

Draw or write one thing you see or hear.

This Reminds Me of . . .

Draw or write what this reminds you of.

Notice and Know Chart

	Sketch what you notice.	Write what you know about what you noticed.
See		
Hear		
Touch		
Feel		

How I Learned About . . .

Write topic name.

Ways to Learn	Draw or write what you know about what you learned.
Playing/ Exploring	
Listening	
Reading	
Watching	

How I Want to Learn About . . .

_____

Write topic name.

Ways to Learn	Draw or write how you want to learn about this topic.
Playing/ Exploring	
Listening	
Reading	
Watching	

STEAM Exploration

Creative Coding Space Race

The previously shared student journal pages and anchor charts in this chapter can be used in many different learning experiences and content areas to help students understand how to make powerful connections. As an additional resource, the following model STEAM exploration will give students an opportunity to delve into a minds-on learning experience while learning to make powerful connections.

Introduction

In this model STEAM exploration, Creative Coding Space Race, students will investigate algorithmic coding. *Algorithmic coding* is likely a new term for most young learners. Opportunities are given for making connections to previous understandings. In this STEAM exploration:

1. Students will learn the word *algorithm* through their current understanding of dressing for the day. We get dressed to solve a problem, and we do so in a particular order.
2. Students will activate schema by completing the innovation journal page *Everything I Know About*, filling in the word *coding* in the blank. This allows them to share things they know that are coded or things that they know are completed in a particular order to solve a problem, like getting dressed. If you see that a child does not have enough schema yet for the word *coding* to tell you what he knows about coding, then use the variation *Everything I Want to Know About*. This still provides you with helpful preassessment information about what the child currently knows and what he wants to know about this topic.
3. Students will then use these experiences and connections as they design their grid and problem solve to complete the coding challenges.

Innovation Focus

Connections

Featured Innovators

Katherine Johnson, Dorothy Vaughan, and Mary Jackson

STEAM Challenge

Katherine Johnson has loved math since she was a very little girl, maybe even younger than you. Now she works for NASA as a human computer! Working alongside her dear friends Dorothy Vaughan (a computer programmer) and Mary Jackson (an engineer), she is solving a challenging problem to help bring an astronaut home safely from space. Are you ready to hear the most exciting part? She has asked for help from a team of young engineers like you! So, what do you say? Are you ready to help solve this coding challenge to bring the astronaut home safely?

STEAM Exploration Materials

- Journal page: *Everything I Know About*
- A stuffed animal or doll with layers of clothing (e.g., shirt, jacket, shoes, pants, hat)
- Activity materials (per small group of 3–6):
  - 1 set of Algorithmic Coding Commands (see p. 46)
  - 10–12 Algorithmic Coding Arrows (see p. 49)
  - Large 25-square grid or gaming board*
  - Astronaut in a spaceship or astronaut/spaceship toy

- Book: *Baby Loves Coding!* by Ruth Spiro
- Book (optional): *Hidden Figures* by Margot Lee Shetterly

* You can create a large grid on a shower curtain by taping or drawing a grid pattern (see Figure 10), or you may purchase a jumbo checkerboard mat. With very young learners you can use a tic-tac-toe grid.

Vocabulary

Algorithm, code, relative location (e.g., above, below, under, on top)

STEAM Exploration Steps

1. Before class, set up the stuffed animal (or doll) coding segment of your lesson. Depending on what items of clothing your animal has, write corresponding sentence strips, such as:
   - Put on shoes.
   - Put on pants.
   - Put on shirt.
   - Put on hat.
   - Put on jacket.

Figure 10. Shower curtain coding grid.

Include illustrations or photographs if your students are not yet readers or are English language learners.

2. To begin the lesson, share a photograph of each NASA innovator and tell students a bit about each person who inspired this STEAM challenge.

   □ **Katherine Johnson.** Katherine loved learning about mathematics from the time she was very young. She graduated college at 18, the age at which most people graduate high school. Katherine was a human computer for NASA and helped put the first American in space and the first man on the moon.

   □ **Dorothy Vaughan.** Dorothy was also a mathematician and one of NASA's first computer programmers. Her work with NASA's early computer programs helped astronauts travel safely in space.

   □ **Mary Jackson.** Like her friends, Mary was one of NASA's human computers, but she was also an important engineer working to design and improve spacecraft. She was the first female African American engineer at NASA.

   Note that these women were pioneers not only in mathematics and science, but also in civil rights. These women made huge scientific advancements during a time when our nation was segregated. They each fought for equality and equity when it was difficult to do so.

3. Share the STEAM challenge with your students (see Appendix: STEAM Challenge Cards). Tell them that they are being asked to develop an algorithmic code to bring an astronaut home! Tell students: *"Algorithmic" sounds like a big word, but you actually work with algorithms every single day. An algorithm is just a series of steps to solve a problem.* Tell your students that when they get dressed, they always follow a series of steps. These steps solve the problem of getting dressed, so these steps are an algorithm. Share the following example of bear coding (see Figure 11).

   □ Place the stuffed animal, items of clothing, and sentence strips where students can see.

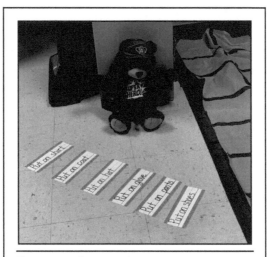

Figure 11. Bear coding.

- ☐ Put the stuffed animal's shoes on and lay out the corresponding sentence strip.
- ☐ Think aloud and attempt to put on the animal's pants. Ask your students: *Why won't the pants go on?* (Because you need to put on pants before shoes.)
- ☐ Have students think about the order in which they get dressed, and have them put the algorithm in the right order. Then, test the algorithm by dressing the bear together.
- ☐ Take a look at the steps and the completely dressed animal. Tell students: *Congrats! You've just completed an algorithm.*

4. Now distribute the innovation journal page *Everything I Know About*. Have students write or draw an image to share everything they know that requires algorithmic steps to complete (e.g., baking a cake, cooking spaghetti, driving a car, putting together LEGO bricks, driving to grandma's house, etc.). This organizer is a great way to activate schema and help children connect to what they know about using procedural steps to solve a problem. Another fun way to record students' connections is to give students sticky notes and have them put a new idea on each note. Then, take their photo with their notes and post all of their connections in the classroom or on a bulletin board. It's a great way for kids to share their innovative thinking and also build community because they can see everyone's ideas.

5. Read aloud *Baby Loves Coding!* by Ruth Spiro. (Teachers of older students, don't be thrown off by the title; this book simplifies the concept of algorithmic coding into language that makes it easy for anyone, from young children to adults, to understand.) If you don't have a copy of this book, or do not think it is appropriate for the levels of your students, take a look at Code.org (https://code.org) as a class. The website offers examples of algorithmic coding to help build schema for learners before they complete this challenge.

6. Show students the large grids that each group will be using for the rest of this activity. If you are working with younger children, you may want to go ahead and tape the astronaut and Earth (home) in the places you want them to be (see the Algorithmic Coding Commands). If you are working with older students, or students who have played these types of games before, you can have them design the game by putting the objects wherever they want.

7. If this is the first time you have done an algorithmic coding activity, model a quick game in whole-group time. Place the astronaut just a few spaces away from Earth and practice together thinking aloud and putting the arrows down to get to Earth. (*Note.* Tic-tac-toe grids are a great way to do a quick model for algorithmic coding with only a few steps. They are also great for young learners who need fewer choices as they build schema for coding.)

8. Have students work in small groups (3–6 students). Each group should have a game board, Algorithmic Coding Arrows, and Algorithmic Coding Commands. Ask students to notice the words they hear one another saying as they decide where to put the arrows. You should hear and model words that describe relative location (i.e., above, below, under, on top).

9. Have students work together to get the astronaut home. Figure 12 shows first-grade students working together to complete this task.

10. As students are working, walk around modeling think alouds that use relative location vocabulary as well as the word *algorithm*. If students need an additional challenge, give them blank paper and have them create their own problems to place around the gameboard. For instance, instead of just going forward or turning, they might say, "radio NASA" or "fix warning light on ship." This makes the process even more creative because students are doing more than following directions; they are actually writing a story.

11. After students are finished, encourage them to view their classmates' game boards to notice if anyone solved the problem differently. As an additional challenge, give students sticky notes and have them list the steps to their algorithm (e.g., go forward 3 times, turn left, go forward 2 times, etc.). They can then post their notes on the floor next to their game board, just as you did with the stuffed animal's clothing directions. If your students are not yet writing, these directions can be created using arrows and numbers rather than words. Lastly, you can also have students clear and reset their game board to make a more challenging space adventure or see if they can make it home using more or fewer commands.

12. There are so many interesting ways to code—algorithmic coding is just one! If your students are still interested in coding, these three activities might be good extensions for them.
    □ Record a top secret message to a friend in Morse code.
    □ Build a letter to a visually impaired friend in braille, using puffy paint or molding sticks.
    □ Create binary necklaces using the binary alphabet code, string, and beads.

Innovation Process Summary

The primary innovation strategy featured in this lesson is connecting. The STEAM exploration shares the real challenge that Katherine Johnson, Dorothy Vaughan, and Mary Jackson faced to help astronauts travel safely in space. Students can then use an algorithmic coding game to bring an astronaut home. Children make connections to help them understand what an algorithm is and to understand how they already solve problems in their day-to-day life by breaking problems into simple parts and steps. Other strategies that may

Figure 12. Coding space race activity.

be useful to point out in this lesson include wondering and reflecting.

Wondering. In this lesson students build schema by thinking about other problems they know how to face, but they will also be wondering as they explore coding. As they are working, you can model statements like, "I wonder if there might be another way to get the astronaut to the Earth." You will also want to listen carefully to students sharing wonderings as they think aloud to problem solve.

Reflecting. As students finish this challenge, reflection should be encouraged. You want children to think about their algorithm and compare it to their classmates'. You may also want them to think about the location of their spaceship and Earth, and reflect to determine if they could create either an easier or a more complex problem to solve. Students should be encouraged to solve any wonderings or redesigns they envision as they are reflecting, even if this learning has to occur on another day.

ALGORITHMIC CODING COMMANDS

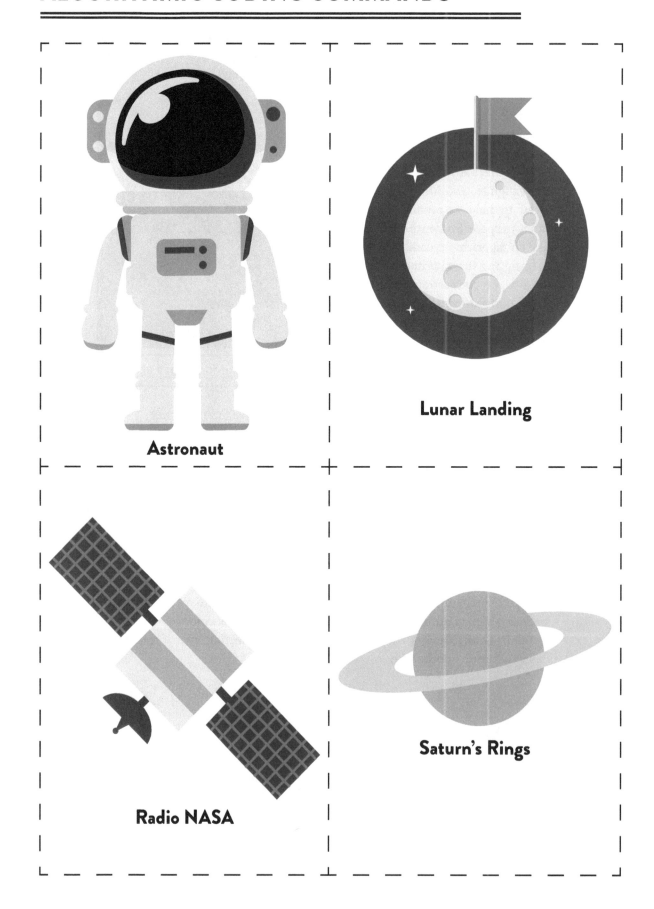

Astronaut

Lunar Landing

Radio NASA

Saturn's Rings

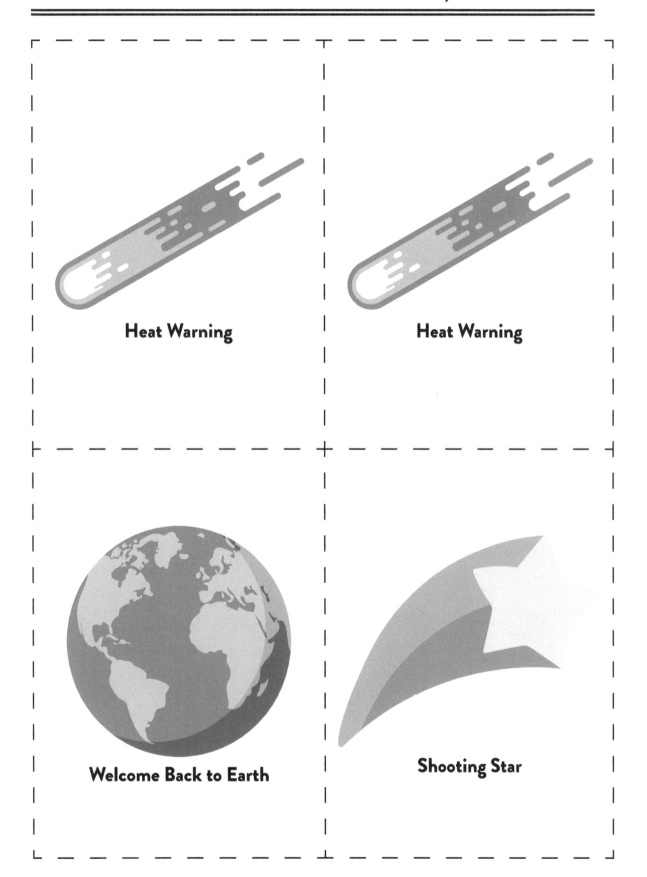

Heat Warning

Heat Warning

Welcome Back to Earth

Shooting Star

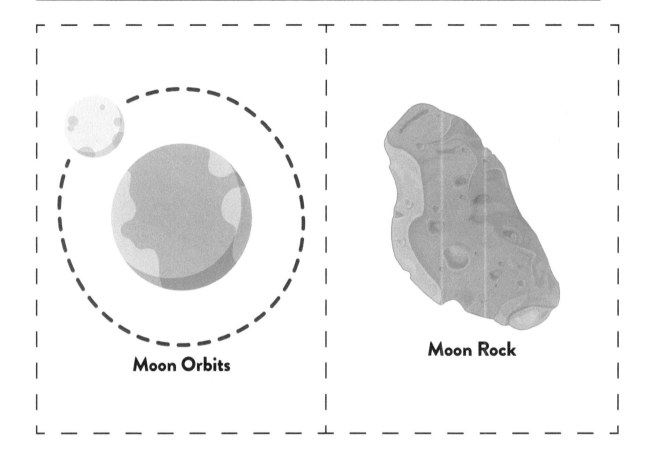

Moon Orbits

Moon Rock

ALGORITHMIC CODING ARROWS

CHAPTER 3

GROWTH MINDSET:
MISTAKE MAKERS = INNOVATORS

"I think I can, I think I can, I think I can . . ." There is a reason why *The Little Engine That Could* is a classic tale for the young and young at heart. Long before *growth mindset* became a buzzword in education, this little engine was used in homes and schools to help teach young learners that they were capable of overcoming challenges to accomplish their goals. What makes an idea stand the test of time like this? Truth.

If we expect our young learners to explore, make mistakes, learn, and try again, we must help them establish a growth mindset. Dweck's (2006) research pioneering this important educational era firmly rooted the term *growth mindset* in the educational vernacular. As educators of young children, we have a responsibility to not only teach children how to see mistakes as an opportunity to grow, but also give them mindfulness strategies to learn to process mistakes and failures. These two tools are powerful when used together to teach stamina and perseverance, important life-ready skills.

How Do Teachers Foster a Growth Mindset?

Although effort is important in establishing growth mindset, it is not the only idea to be considered. In 2015, Dweck revisited her work on mindset and added a few points of clarification:

> Perhaps the most common misconception is simply equating the growth mindset with effort. Certainly, effort is key for students' achievement, but it's not the only thing. Students need to try new strategies and seek input from others when they're stuck. They need this repertoire of approaches—not just sheer effort—to learn and improve. . . . When they're stuck, teachers can appreciate their work so far, but add: "Let's talk about what you've tried, and what you can try next." (para. 5)

Encourage students to play, learn, and explore, but most importantly, teach them to make mistakes. Mistakes are how the very best learning takes place. Teach children to say, "Oops . . . I learned . . ." to help remember that mistakes are just a stepping stone on the path to innovation.

As teachers of young learners, we lay the foundation for helping them understand how to deal with frustration and recognize mistakes as a start to learning. No matter your age, making mistakes and moving forward can be tough. The following are a few ideas of things you can do to encourage innovative and creative thinking.

- **Share literature and other media that model growth mindset and moving forward.** When young learners are reading or listening to a book, they feel those characters' experiences. Introduce them to this idea through an engaging book. Then, when your students make a mistake in class, reflect back on that text. When working with your youngest learners, the book *Beautiful Oops!* by Barney Saltzberg is phenomenal in its use of art to model this concept. It completely changed the mindset in my classroom, as my students began calling all mistakes a "beautiful oops" on their own. *The Dot* and *Ish* by Peter H. Reynolds are other great resources for modeling this concept with students.
- **After a mistake, always, always, always ask what the student has learned.** Simply telling children that you expect them to make mistakes is not enough. If we want to hold students (and ourselves as teachers) accountable for growth mindset, we must always ask students what they've learned after a mistake. "What did you learn from that?" and "What will you try differently next time?" should be such common phrases in our classrooms that students begin to parrot them.
- **Share what didn't work, too—not only the right answer.** This simple strategy completely changed my classroom. I had found that students

were hesitant to make mistakes. What was worse, my students often resented the student who "figured it out" first when they were working through a challenge. It was detrimental to our classroom environment. By changing the way students shared their findings, I flipped the importance. When I only had students share the right answer, that was the only thing my students saw as important. By adding in the expectation that students would share what they tried that *didn't* work, students began to see that I valued their efforts, perseverance, and the various thinking strategies it took to solve a problem. In addition, students who may not have "figured it out" yet began to see that their mistakes were a path to learning; they realized that they had tried many of the same strategies as the student who eventually found the answer.

- **Make use of mindfulness tools in the classroom to support growth mindset.** A lot of emphasis has been put on the terms *growth mindset* and *mindfulness* in school, but we don't often see how interrelated they are. These two ideas must be used in combination in order to grow young minds. Simply telling a young learner to move on from a mistake is not enough. Mistakes come with big emotions that little learners don't often know how to process. We must give them the tools they need to process, calm down, and move on from these emotions (see Chapter 1 for more mindfulness strategies).

Journaling and Anchor Charts: Growth Mindset

The following can be used as anchor charts or as student journal pages to record thinking as children explore growth mindset and the notion of learning from mistakes.

- *Oops . . . I Learned*: This journal encourages students to notice a mistake they have made while exploring or learning and share what they learned from this mistake. It can be completed with words, drawings, or both depending on the needs of the student. (This journal page is also used in this chapter's sample STEAM exploration.)
- *Not Yet, But Almost!*: Students will use this tool to journal about the almost-correct answer or the experiment that worked for just a moment before it failed. Teachers can also use this as an anchor chart to clarify common misconceptions that students may have, especially if students are making similar mistakes as they investigate a topic.
- *The Best Mistake We Made*: This is a variation of the two previous tools listed. This tool is unique because it is made specifically for pairs or groups of students. Students will work together to draw and/or write about a mistake they've made, and also share what they learned from the mistake by sharing why it was the best mistake.
- *Growing My Mind*: This tool works well as a student journal or anchor chart for the class; students can continually add to it as they learn new information. It serves as a visual reminder that the child's mind is always growing.

Oops . . .

Draw or write about your mistake here.

I Learned . . .

Share what you learned from your mistake here.

Not Yet, But Almost!

Hooray, you haven't solved it *yet*, but you're almost there.

Draw or write about one thing that worked or one thing you learned in your exploration.

Draw or write about what you plan to do next.

The Best Mistake We Made

Draw or write about something in your group's exploration that didn't go as planned.

Share two things your mistake helped you learn.

Growing My Mind

On each tree, draw or write one thing you learned.

STEAM Exploration

Creative Chemistry Lab

The student journal pages and anchor charts shared in this chapter can be used in many different learning experiences and content areas to help students understand how to learn from mistakes. As an additional resource, this model STEAM exploration, Creative Chemistry Lab, will give students an opportunity to delve into a minds-on learning experience while exploring growth mindset.

Introduction

Sticky notes, Play-Doh, Silly Putty, Band-Aids, chocolate chip cookies—each of these things were created by accident! These popular creations are a perfect way to introduce young learners to the notion of growth mindset because they illustrate the power of perseverance and seeing an idea in a new light. Although this lesson, in particular, features an invention that was created from a failure, each and every STEAM investigation in this book (and beyond) should offer an opportunity for children to make mistakes and move forward. If students are working at the right level of challenge, this process is an organic part of learning. In the Creative Chemistry Lab STEAM exploration:

1. Students will learn about real-world examples of failures that became successes through perseverance and creative thinking.
2. Students will explore sequence of events, measurement, and physical properties as they create their own playdough.
3. Students will share an "Oops . . . I learned" moment and practice mindfulness strategies as needed as they brainstorm and create an innovative use for the playdough created in this exploration.

Innovation Focus

Growth mindset

Featured Accidental Inventions

Play-Doh, Silly Putty

STEAM Challenge

Chocolate chip cookies, Silly Putty, Slinky, sticky notes, Play-Doh, Band-Aids—did you know that these things were all invented by accident? It's true! Noah McVicker was working in his family's soap company when he accidentally invented Play-Doh. Silly Putty was created by accident, too. Now it's marketed as a toy, but did you know that it has been used by astronauts in space to hold their tools down in zero gravity? Young innovators, you are challenged to recreate play-dough in our Creative Chemistry Lab. Then, you will put on your creative thinking caps and create a new use for this accidental invention, just like astronauts discovered that Silly Putty could hold objects in space!

STEAM Exploration Materials

- Student journal page: *Oops . . . I Learned*
- Playdough (per small group of 2–6):
    - 2 cups flour
    - 1 cup salt
    - 1 tbsp vegetable oil
    - 1 cup water
    - 10–12 drops food coloring

- Gallon-size zipper plastic bags (1 per group)
- Measuring cups
- Tablespoons
- Plastic table covers
- Magnifying glasses or age-appropriate microscope
- Safety goggles and lab coats
- Loose parts lab: chenille stems, craft sticks, buttons/beads, construction paper

Vocabulary

Physical characteristics, properties

STEAM Exploration Steps

1. Share the story of Play-Doh with your students: *In the 1930s, Noah McVicker was working in his family's lab and accidently created a putty. His family noticed it could clean wallpaper and decided to sell it. Eventually, people stopped buying it to clean, and McVicker's company turned its attention to*

only liquid cleaners. Ask students how they think Noah probably felt when people stopped buying the putty he invented. Ask students if they have ever felt disappointed like Noah.

2. Continue the story: *Noah eventually learned from his brother that teachers were purchasing the putty and using it for craft projects for their students. McVicker's company learned of this and decided to sell the putty as a toy for kids. Play-Doh was born!* Remind students that Noah likely felt frustrated when he learned the company was abandoning his invention. Ask them why it was important that he was willing to change his thinking about his invention. (He was able to create a toy rather than a cleaning supply.)

3. Share the playdough challenge with students (see Appendix: STEAM Challenge Cards). Share the recipe for playdough. See Figure 13 for the recipe ingredients and steps. For visual learners or soon-to-be readers, remember to include pictures with each step; see Figure 14 for an example.

4. Have students look at the recipe for playdough. Ask them what this recipe reminds them of. It will likely remind students of how they created steps for algorithmic coding to help guide an astronaut to Earth in Chapter 2.

5. Welcome students to the Creative Chemistry Lab!
   □ Distribute goggles and lab coats.
   □ Cover the tables in plastic table coverings.
   □ Include a magnifying glass or age-appropriate microscope on the table for students to look closely at the ingredients and their properties before they mix them.
   □ Have students follow the directions on the recipe to create playdough.
   □ *Note.* You can premeasure ingredients for younger children into individual containers, or work with them in small groups to measure and create the playdough. Older students or students with prior experience with this type of investigation might be ready to measure their own ingredients. Do whichever option is better for your young learners. Either way, be sure to talk about the quantity of each ingredient. This is good exposure to numeracy for younger students. Older students would benefit from some problem-solving questions (e.g., If this recipe makes enough playdough for two people, how many cups of salt will we need for the whole class of 22 students?).

6. Working in small groups, have students create the playdough (see Figure 15). As students add each ingredient, have them discuss the physical properties of that ingredient:
   □ color,
   □ shape,
   □ size,
   □ state of matter (e.g., solid, liquid), and
   □ texture.

How to Make Playdough

Ingredients

- 2 cups flour
- 1 cup salt
- 1 tbsp vegetable oil
- 1 cup water
- 10–12 drops food coloring

Steps

1. Add flour and salt to resealable bag.
2. Mix well by kneading the bag.
3. Add water, food coloring, and oil.
4. Mix well by kneading the bag.
5. Take the dough out of the bag and knead it.
6. Give the playdough a test. If it is too wet, sprinkle in a little more flour. If it is too dry, add a few drops of water. If the playdough is just right, it's time to explore!

Figure 13. Playdough recipe.

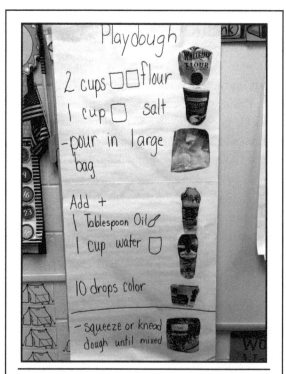

Figure 14. Playdough recipe with pictures.

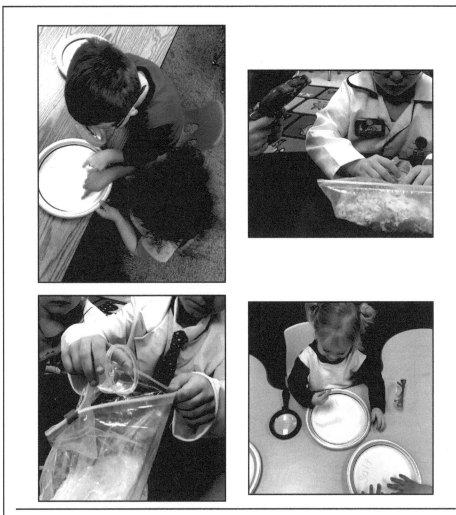

Figure 15. Playdough chemistry lab.

7. Have students help you clean up any mess left behind from creating the playdough.

8. Give students time to explore and play with their playdough. Have them continue wearing their safety equipment to model lab-appropriate behavior.

9. Remind students that Silly Putty is used in space to hold tools. Tell them this works for astronauts because Silly Putty is a little sticky, and its properties allow it to mold into different shapes. What properties does playdough have? As a class, create a list of physical properties of the playdough that students created. Discuss how these properties are different than the properties of each of the individual ingredients. Ask students to think about these properties and how the playdough they created may help solve a problem, just like the astronauts used Silly Putty to hold their tools in space. For example, playdough is moldable into different shapes, which might allow it to work as a gripper for a different writing tool.

10. Introduce students to the loose parts lab: a tray of craft sticks, chenille stems, construction paper, and large buttons or beads. Tell students that they are welcome to use these craft materials to help them think about how they may use their playdough in a new way.

11. Tell students that playdough was created from an "Oops . . . I learned" moment. Noah McVicker's statement may have been: *Oops, I meant to create a cleaner, but I learned that my invention worked well for crafts!* Have students share an "Oops . . . I learned" moment in their exploration. Let them know that you expect that they will try something that doesn't work exactly how they want it to, and that's great. It means they are learning!

12. Have students explore further, working in pairs or small groups to brainstorm another use for playdough. For example, a student in Tracy Tharp's kindergarten class designed a headphone holder (see Figure 16).

13. As students are working, walk around and listen for their "Oops . . . I learned" statements. Help them model saying the phrase as you see them learning from trial and error.

14. If you notice that students are frustrated with their attempts and mistakes, remind them to use their mindfulness strategies. This would be a good opportunity to share the Turtle Breathing (Take 5) mindfulness strategy (see p. 19).

15. When they finish creating and exploring, have students record their discoveries in their *Oops . . . I Learned* innovation journals or on a class anchor chart. Give students time to share their innovation or invention with small groups or the whole class.

Innovation Process Summary

The primary innovation strategy featured in this lesson is growth mindset. The STEAM challenge shares the real-world examples of failures that became useful inventions. This lesson also gives children an opportunity to learn from their own failures as they brainstorm other uses for the playdough they create. Students can also practice growth mindset by using mindfulness strategies as a part of their chemistry lab. Other strategies that may be useful to point out in this lesson include connecting and empathy.

Connecting. In this lesson, students build connections to previous learning by comparing the recipe to the steps in the algorithmic coding lesson.

Empathy. Another important component in this lesson is empathy. Students are asked to put themselves in the mistake maker's shoes (i.e., think about how Noah McVicker felt when he was told that his innovation wasn't going to be used). Students also need to think about how to take those feelings and move forward. The ability to keep going or persist, even when you are frustrated, is an important part of learning with a growth mindset.

Figure 16. Student invention using playdough.

INSPIRING INNOVATION AND CREATIVITY IN YOUNG LEARNERS

FAMILY
RESOURCES PAGES

SUMMER STEAM
BUCKET LIST

1. Make ice cream in a bag.

2. Create a toy boat from recycled materials.

3. On a clear night, go on a constellation hunt.

4. Create a pizza box solar oven and make s'mores.

5. Help plan a "staycation" day trip.

FALL STEAM
BUCKET LIST

1. Go on a leaf hunt! Find as many different kinds as possible.

2. Make popcorn dance by putting a few kernels in different sodas.

3. Potion lab: Explore with baking soda, vinegar, and food coloring.

4. Make your favorite gooey slime.

5. Visit an orchard or farm.

WINTER STEAM BUCKET LIST

1. Snowball fight! Create a catapult for cotton balls.

2. Create your own adventurous place to hibernate (for example, a castle, igloo, or rocket) using a large recycled box.

3. Catch snowflakes on frozen black paper and observe with a magnifying glass.

4. Explore why we salt the roads in winter. Freeze a toy car and use rock salt to help melt the ice.

5. Record a valentine message in Morse code for a friend.

SPRING STEAM BUCKET LIST

1. Create three shakers that have a unique sound, using plastic eggs, rice, cereal, and beans.

2. Create a chromatography rainbow with a coffee filter, water, and a black water-based marker. Color the coffee filter, spray with water, and watch the rainbow appear!

3. Explore outside with bubbles. Bubbles = 6 parts water to 1 part dish soap.

4. Dissect a seed or a flower. Explore what you see with a magnifying glass.

5. Create a habitat for a pet rock, fairy, or gnome.

LITTLE LEARNERS BUCKET LIST

1.

2.

3.

4.

5.

10 THINGS
to Ask Instead of "What Did You Learn?"

1. What did this remind you of?

2. What did you try that didn't work?

3. What made you smile/laugh?

4. Who did you learn with today?
   Tell me about what you explored together.

5. What do you wonder now?

6. What did you notice (see, hear, feel)?

7. If you could change something that happened, what would that be?

8. What was the best thing about . . . ?

9. What was the most important thing about . . . ?

10. What helped you keep going when you felt frustrated?

CHAPTER 4

EMPATHY MAKES LEARNING MATTER

When Easton LaChappelle was 14 years old he built a robotic hand using LEGO bricks. After meeting a 7-year-old girl with a prosthetic arm, this young man used 3-D printing to reduce the cost of artificial limb technology by tens of thousands of dollars. Anna Stork and Andrea Sreshta were in college when they were inspired by the needs of the victims of a devastating earthquake in Haiti. Together in a studio class they invented the prototype of an inflatable solar-powered lantern called LuminAID that could be distributed to those in need. The initial model of LuminAID was created from a plastic bag, a solar panel, and a sports bottle cap. After several tests and redesigns, this innovation has now helped thousands of victims of natural disasters.

What do both of these stories have in common? Empathy. In both of these examples, young adults were inspired to think creatively to help solve the problems of someone in need. Empathy is so much more powerful that sympathy. With sympathy, the observer says, "bless your heart" and moves on with his life. However, when we teach students about the power of empathy and what it means to feel and truly understand another's situation, problem solving becomes meaningful.

How Do Teachers Foster Empathy?

Empathy is at the heart of innovation; therefore, it is imperative that young learners have opportunities to listen and learn from the experiences of others. The ability to make connections to their own learning experiences will help young learners think about how others feel. Finding a problem that matters to young learners can be the ticket to engaging them in a meaningful problem-based learning experience.

Teachers of young learners are challenged with the important task of showing students how to move from sympathy to empathy. No matter their age, kids are capable of being world changers, or at the very least, they are capable of dreaming of how they will change the world when they grow up. The following are a few ideas of things you can do to encourage empathy in innovative and creative thinking.

- **Share literature and real-life stories of problems that others are solving.** Point out to students the difference between sympathy and empathy.
- **Develop schema in students.** Schema, or the ability to connect new content to students' previous experiences, is very important in empathy. Through experiencing and understanding their own emotions, children can learn how to feel empathy for others. Therefore, the issues that young learners often feel the most empathetic about, and inspired to solve, will originate from problems they have faced themselves, emotions they have felt, or something someone very close to them has experienced. This is great! Go with it. Every empathetic experience students have only builds more schema for them to connect to later in life.
- **Provide feedback.** If you notice that students in your classroom are empathetic to others' needs and help to solve others' problems, give them specific feedback to let them know what they've done to be world changers. These little deeds and choices every day make the world a better place. Specific feedback on this is meaningful to students.
- **Listen to your students.** Notice what they seem passionate about and help them harness that energy into problem solving. Maybe they are upset that the playground doesn't have enough equipment for children who have motor skills impairments. Perhaps they worry that not all students can fit into the restrooms during a tornado drill. Whatever bothers them is the ticket to engaging them. It is also the perfect opportunity to have them make a plan for how to help others. Keep Makerspace materials nearby and available to help make it easy for children to create and problem solve. You never know when empathy will inspire you or your students.

Journaling and Anchor Charts: Empathy

The following can be used as anchor charts or student journal pages as students explore the concept of empathy and learn how to use it to inspire creative thinking and innovation.

- *It Bothers Me When*: This is a student journal page that allows students to draw, write, or both about topics and problems that concern them. This will help students identify problems that they would like to solve.

- *When I Grow Up, I Want to Solve This Problem*: This variation of the previous tool asks children what problem they want to solve when they get older, rather than who they want to be or what career they would like to pursue. (This student journal page is used in the sample STEAM exploration included in this chapter.)

- *Interviews for Empathy*: Students have the opportunity to brainstorm and interview others about a problem that they would like to solve. These interviews will help children develop empathy and a greater understanding of the problem. It also offers a great mathematics connection with data and analysis.

- *Make It Better, Mini-Maker!*: This anchor chart or student journal page will work well for older children. It is a sketch note that takes students through the thinking process for identifying a problem and creating something in a Makerspace to solve that problem.

It Bothers Me When . . .

Draw or write about a problem that bothers you.

Here's what
I think I can do to help . . .

When I Grow Up, I Want to Solve This Problem . . .

Draw or write about who you would like to help.

How Will You Help?

Draw or write about the problem you would like to help solve.

Interviews for Empathy

Write three questions you will ask others to help you better understand the problem.

1. _____

2. _____

3. _____

How will you collect your data? _____

Who will help you understand this problem? Name three people you plan to interview.

1. _____

2. _____

3. _____

After you have reviewed your data, share at least one big idea you learned to help you solve this problem.

Make It Better, Mini-Maker!

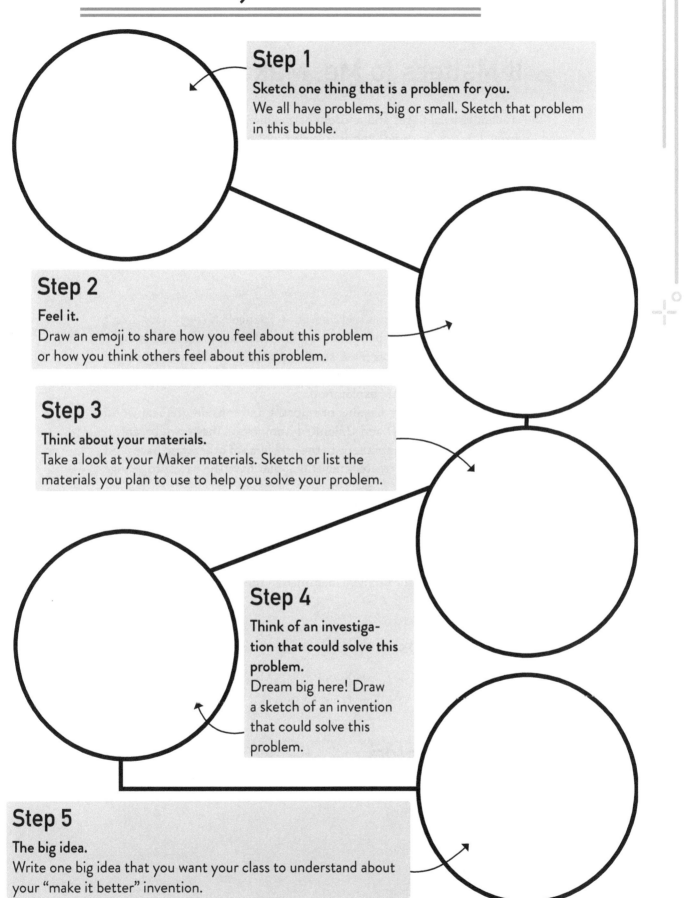

Step 1

Sketch one thing that is a problem for you.
We all have problems, big or small. Sketch that problem in this bubble.

Step 2

Feel it.
Draw an emoji to share how you feel about this problem or how you think others feel about this problem.

Step 3

Think about your materials.
Take a look at your Maker materials. Sketch or list the materials you plan to use to help you solve your problem.

Step 4

Think of an investigation that could solve this problem.
Dream big here! Draw a sketch of an invention that could solve this problem.

Step 5

The big idea.
Write one big idea that you want your class to understand about your "make it better" invention.

STEAM Exploration

It Matters to Me: Makerspace

The student journal pages and anchor charts shared in this chapter can be used in many different learning experiences and content areas to help students understand empathy and how it can inspire innovation and creative thinking. As an additional resource, this model STEAM exploration will give students an opportunity to delve into a minds-on Makerspace showcasing empathy as the innovation strategy.

Introduction

Jaime Casap (2019), Google's Chief Education Evangelist, suggested, "Don't ask kids what they want to be when they grow up. Ask what problem they want to solve." (For more videos on this topic, see Casap's YouTube channel at https://www.youtube.com/jaimecasap.) The mini-Makerspace shared in this chapter is built on this idea. In this STEAM exploration:

1. Students will learn the meaning of empathy and consider the real-world examples of LuminAID and Unlimited Tomorrow. These two organizations' founders were empathetic to the problems of others and have used their STEAM skills to create innovations that have the power to change the world.
2. Students will complete the innovation journal page modeled after Casap's (2019) quote, *When I Grow Up, I Want to Solve This Problem*, identifying a problem they would like to solve.
3. Students will plan, design, and create a prototype or model of an innovation that will solve the problem identified in their empathy journal.

Innovation Focus

Empathy

Featured Innovators

Anna Stork and Andrea Sreshta (LuminAID), Easton LaChappelle (robotic arm, Unlimited Tomorrow, Inc.)

STEAM Challenge

You are never too young to be a world changer! Anna Stork and Andrea Sreshta were in college when they noticed that people needed help after a devastating earthquake. They wanted to help bring light to those in need, so with a simple solar panel, a plastic bag, and a sports bottle cap, they invented a light to help people see when there is no electricity after a natural disaster. Easton LaChappelle wanted to help people who couldn't use their hands. He was only 14 when he designed a robotic hand using LEGO bricks! What do Anna, Andrea, and Easton have in common? They each had a problem they wanted to solve and the heart to help. Now, they have a challenge for you. What problem do you want to solve? Put on your innovator eyes and your hardworking hands, because today you will have the chance to create your own innovation to solve a problem that is heavy on your heart.

Vocabulary

Empathy, model, prototype

STEAM Exploration Materials

- Student journal page: *When I Grow Up, I Want to Solve This Problem*
- Book(s): *Not a Box* and/or *Not a Stick* by Antoinette Portis
- Graph paper
- Mini-Makerspace materials*
    - Various sizes of boxes and/or sticks (dowel rods will also work)
    - Hole punches
    - Foam board, golf tee, and child-safe mallet (for punching holes that a hole punch cannot reach; see p. 122 for a photo example)
    - Scissors
    - Construction paper
    - Glue or tape
    - Chenille stems, craft sticks, straws, aluminum foil
    - Plastic zipper bags or paper cups
    - LEGO bricks

* The sky's the limit here on supplies. Use as many or as few as you are comfortable with. You can have children collect items on nature walks or bring in items from home. Or you can keep it simple and provide them only a few choices. This activity is a good one for using any recycled items in your classroom. These materials will be used in a mini-Makerspace to design students' invention/innovation.

STEAM Exploration Steps

1. Ask your students: *Isn't it inspiring to know that you can change the world?* Review the three innovators' stories from the challenge (see Appendix: STEAM Challenge Cards), ensuring that students understand how the inventions solved a problem the inventor was interested in.

2. For this lesson, children will use the *When I Grow Up, I Want to Solve This Problem* journal page or prompt. It is often helpful to build some schema first, because identifying a problem you want to solve can be challenging for young learners. There are two ways to do this.
   - Ask students to take some time to think about people they know and the problems those people solve. Examples might include: Dr. Smith (pediatrician) wants to help young children feel better when their ears hurt; Mrs. Jamie (humane society director) wants to help animals without a place to live find forever homes; Mr. James (physical therapist) wants to help children learn to walk and run.
   - Ask students to look at everyday objects and the problem these objects solve (e.g., the alarm app on the phone solves the problem of oversleeping; the stoplight solves the problem of traffic accidents).

3. Share the word *empathy* with your students, as this will likely be a new word for them. Tell them: *Empathy is when we really try to understand what it feels like to be someone else. This is different from a word that sounds similar,* sympathy. *Sympathy means we just feel sad for someone else, but empathy goes beyond feeling sad. Empathy has the power to make you a world changer.* Review the innovators' projects and identify who the innovators felt empathy for (i.e., people living where natural disasters occur, people without a working arm or hand).

4. Tell students that adults have had it wrong for years. Adults ask kids what they want to be when they group up, but there's actually a much better question that great young thinkers like them can answer instead. Jaime Casap (2019), an educational innovator who works for Google, said that we shouldn't ask what kids want to be; we should ask what problem they want to solve.

5. Now it's time for your little learners to think about the big problems they want to solve. You can facilitate this discussion by having students do the following process with each question: thinking independently, partner talking, and then writing or drawing their responses on the *When I Grow Up, I Want to Solve This Problem* journal page, or in their innovation notebook. See Figure 17 for one student's example.
   - Who or what would you like to help (e.g., children, adults, animals, plants)?
   - What are problems these people/animals/plants face that bother you?

6. Read aloud the book *Not a Box* and/or *Not a Stick* by Antoinette Portis. After reading about each invention the character makes, stop and discuss what problem was solved (e.g., the rocket might help scientists study space; a fishing pole might help feed the hungry).

7. Share the mini-Makerspace materials with students and have them reread or share the problem they want to solve when they are grown up. Give students time to plan how they will use a box or stick and the additional materials to create a model of an invention or innovation to solve that problem. Note that we call

Figure 17. When I grow up response.

it a model (or prototype, for older children) because it may not have all of the working parts to make it function exactly as it would in real life. However, students can use their Makerspace materials and imagination to create symbols for those items. So, if a child is creating a device to help young children speak, she may use a black paper plate decorated with squares to represent a solar panel to power the device. Examples of completed prototypes can be found in Figure 18. However, on that same note, if you are working with older children and want to include circuitry or robotics concepts and materials, this would be a perfect opportunity to do so.

8. Remind your young learners that what they create does not have to be a brand-new invention. Easton LaChappelle didn't invent the robotic arm; he made it more affordable. This is true of Thomas Edison, also. He didn't invent the light bulb, but he improved it and made it affordable.

9. Distribute graph paper and have students draw a model of their design before they begin, including the available materials they will need.

10. Tell students that Easton LaChappelle (2019) said, "Creativity is the key to innovation!" Tell students you expect them to think outside of the box and make mistakes as they learn and explore. Give your little learners time to explore, share, and create. Students may take more than one class period to plan, create, and share their innovations. See Figure 19 for examples of students working in mini-Makerspaces in the classroom.

11. After students have completed their project, be sure they have time to share the following ideas about their invention:
    □ who they are helping,
    □ the problem they wanted to solve, and
    □ how their innovation helps to solve this problem.

Figure 18. Completed prototypes (a self-inflating soccer ball and a water re-freezer for arctic polar bears).

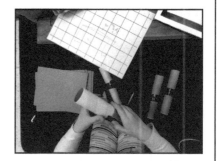

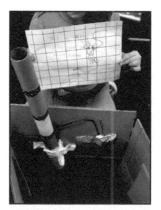

Figure 19. Students working in mini-Makerspaces.

Innovation Process Summary

The primary innovation strategy featured in this lesson is empathy. The STEAM challenge shares examples of young people who have felt empathy for others and created something to improve their lives. This process is then replicated in the Makerspace activity that children are doing as they work to solve a problem of their choosing. As with previous lessons, empathy is not the only strategy used in this lesson. Students will naturally move through most, if not all, of the strategies that encourage innovation and creativity. Other strategies that may be useful to point out in this lesson include connecting and inference.

Connecting. In this lesson, we build schema by asking students to think about grown-ups they know and the problems they solve each day. We also have students think about everyday objects or technologies they use and what problems they were created to solve.

Inference. Although inference is not explicitly taught in this lesson, it is definitely an important part of this mini-Makerspace. Inference requires students to see something, think about what they know about that topic/object, and think of what that means. Students will be evaluating several materials, and then making inferences as they plan and create how to use those items in new or different ways in their designs.

CHAPTER 5

WONDER AND CURIOSITY

A child's wonder is the almost magical component that drives play-based learning. It is a powerful tool that should be nurtured and continually developed. Almost as soon as language progresses in young learners, they are asking questions: *Why is the sky blue? How do we make cookies? Why isn't my birthday every week?* The world is new to our young learners, and their curiosity guides not only language, but also play-based explorations. Young children knock down blocks because they want to know what makes them fall. They mix different paints to see how the color changes. They jump on the bed to see how it's different than the floor. Young learners are scientists. However, in the early years of education, we hold a fragile opportunity in our hands; we can either kindle that flame to continue to spark curiosity and exploration, or we can snuff it out with a teacher-directed approach to learning. There is no better way to inspire authentic learning than to let a child's wondering be the guide.

How Do Teachers Foster Wonder and Curiosity?

A Littlewoods Retailer survey from Australia revealed that young children ask on average 228 questions per day (News.com.au, 2013). Teachers and family members of young children are probably not surprised by this number; however, a more alarming number comes next. The same survey found that the number of questions per day posed by 9-year-olds was only 144. The number of questions was cut in half. The assumption is that the older the child becomes, the fewer questions he or she asks. We do not want this to happen. Some would argue that young children are simply exposed to more new material due to their lack of schema and age. Although that point may be true, shouldn't children continue to be exposed to new and exciting material as they age? Of course, they should. As educators, our job is to share information and materials that keep students challenged and curious. The following are a few ideas of things you can do to encourage wonder in innovative and creative thinking.

- **Listen to what inspires curiosity in children.** If you hear them ask a question or wonder about something, make a note of that. Knowing topics that engage thinking in students opens the door to innovation. You can also seek out this information by doing a preassessment journaling activity asking students for all of the things they wonder about a particular topic (see journal page *Wonderings Circling Around in My Mind*).

- **Materials matter!** Give students access to materials to explore. They need materials for measuring, recording their thinking, and just sparking interest that will make them wonder. Great examples are blocks (for very young students), LEGO bricks (for older students), age-appropriate microscopes with blank slides, and magnifying glasses. Wonder can happen anywhere, but we can spark this feeling by having materials of interest for exploration readily available for our students. On that same note, because children are still developing executive function skills, too many materials can be a distraction.

- **Give students choice.** As children get older or have more schema for innovative explorations, they can handle and make choices with more materials. Younger students, or students who have had limited opportunities for innovative explorations, will perform better when offered only a few choices. The important thing is choice itself. When students are choosing whether to use a chenille stem or a strip of paper, they must think about the properties of each of those objects and then test the objects. Choice in materials encourages deeper thinking, but students don't need a million items available to do this type of thinking. So, provide opportunities for choice in materials, but know your learners and do what is best for them.

- **Outline safety expectations for play-based learning.** Because their brains are still developing, young learners may not accurately be able to determine when an exploration could lead to a harmful outcome. Let children wonder and test. Encourage curiosity and exploring. However, make sure you have your classroom management safety expectations in place. Ensure that students understand that some things must be tested with an adult nearby, and you would love to wonder and explore with them. Have safety equipment readily available for children to use, but set the expectation that they must check in with you first. For example, if a child wants to create something on the playground and wants to use the safety goggles, you can set the expectation that he must see you for those goggles before he can use them. This expectation is not designed to keep the goggles away from students; instead it will ensure that students discuss their explorations with you before they happen. A common misconception is that students are in complete control in a student-centered environment. Although children do have a lot of freedom to explore, the teacher is still the guide. The teacher ensures that students are safe and makes choices about the initial materials available to explore and the types of questions posed. In this way, the teacher is still shaping the experiences in a student-centered environment.

- **Remember that wonder and curiosity do not have a beginning or an ending.** As students build more schema, it is natural that they will make more observations and should, in turn, ask more questions. A widely shared saying states, "Education is not the filling of a pail, but the lighting of a fire!" This fire sparks even more wondering questions. Some of the best "I wonders" will come at the end of an exploration. This makes learning a cycle, and it is also what makes wondering a powerful tool for reflection.

Journaling and Anchor Charts: Wonder and Curiosity

The following can be used as anchor charts or student journal pages to record thinking as students wonder and explore.

- *Wonderings Circling Around in My Mind*: In this organizer, students will jot down or draw all of the things they wonder about a particular topic.
- *Notice and Wonder Chart*: Similar to the *Notice and Know Chart* (see Chapter 2), this chart gives students the opportunity to share what they notice and also write down or draw to communicate what they wonder about that observation.
- *One Thing That Lit My Fire!*: This tool allows students the opportunity to wonder and reflects on the learning for the day. Students will write or draw something that "lit their fire" or made them excited that day, and then share how they can learn more about that topic.
- *I Noticed, I Wonder*. Similar to the notice and wonder chart above, this variation allows children to note an observation and then share what they wonder. This variation works well for children who are younger or just learning to journal. (This journal page is featured in the following model STEAM exploration for this chapter.)

Wonderings Circling Around in My Mind

_____

Write topic name.

Notice and Wonder Chart

	Sketch what you notice.	Write what you wonder about it.
See		
Hear		
Touch		
Feel		

One Thing That Lit My Fire!

I Can Learn More About It by . . .

Education is not the filling of a pail, but the lighting of a fire!

I Noticed . . .

Draw or write to describe what you learned from your exploration.

I Wonder . . .

Draw or write what you wonder about now.

Wonder Workshop: Flying Toys

The student journal pages and anchor charts shared in this chapter can be used in many different learning experiences and content areas to help students begin to understand how wondering is an important part of the innovation process. As an additional resource, this model STEAM exploration will give students an opportunity to wonder and explore as they think creatively and innovate.

Introduction

Temple Grandin is a world-famous innovator in humanely raising livestock and a renowned speaker in the areas of animal behavior and autism spectrum disorders. Grandin is twice-exceptional, meaning that she has a unique gift and ability but also a special need. Although she didn't learn to speak until she was 3 and struggled with bullying and school, she overcome those obstacles and became a very successful and inspiring innovator. Students should be exposed to diversity in the innovators they study. This allows children to see themselves as innovators by connecting to the characteristics of other unique individuals. This point was made evident when special education teachers Charley Jo Allen and Robin Lee cotaught an exploration. While reading a children's biography on Grandin, *The Girl Who Thought in Pictures*, a student called out, "Hey, I think she has autism like me! I think in pictures, too!" This is exactly what we want to happen for students. Thinking back to the *Draw an Innovator* preassessment in the Chapter 1, we want each student to begin to see him- or herself as an innovator. Through exposure to diverse innovators, this will begin to happen for your students.

When Grandin was a very young child, she was curious. One kind of toy she loved to play with and create was a bird kite. She wondered: If she bent the wings of a bird kite, would it fly higher? It did! Wondering, curiosity, and exploring led the way to Grandin's success later in life. The investigation in this lesson is based off of Grandin's examples of bird kites. Students will be given materials to make a different type of flying toy and will be asked to let their wondering guide their unique designs, just as Grandin did. In this STEAM exploration:

1. Students will read or listen to *The Girl Who Thought in Pictures*, a picture book about Temple Grandin. In this text they will learn not only how curiosity inspired innovation for Grandin, but also how she persevered to become an innovator. The book also features a letter written to students from Grandin. Students can write back to her at https://www.temple grandin.com.

2. Students will ask a wondering question to guide their investigation using the *I Noticed, I Wonder* journal page. (For your youngest learners, you can replace the word *notice* with the sensory word that matches your activity—e.g., *see, hear*.)

3. Students will determine important ideas about what makes a successful flying toy.
4. Students will plan, design, and create a flying toy using their wondering.

Innovation Focus

Wonder

Featured Innovator

Temple Grandin

STEAM Challenge

Young Temple loves to create and fly her bird kites out of old scraps of paper. Last week she wondered if a kite would fly differently if she folded the wings. After some fun exploring and playing outside, she learned that it did—the kite flew higher with bent wings! Now, she can't stop wondering if there are other ways to make toys that fly. She wanted to make a new bird kite but doesn't have any paper large enough. All she can find are some strips of paper and plastic straws. Temple wonders if it's possible to turn that trash into flying treasure. What do you say, young engineer? Will you explore to help Temple design the best flying toy possible?

Vocabulary

Gravity, thrust, lift, drag, height, distance, durability

STEAM Exploration Materials

- Student journal page: *I Noticed, I Wonder*
- Book: *The Girl Who Thought in Pictures* by Julia Finley Mosca
- Book (optional): *Rocket Science for Babies* by Chris Ferrie
- Strips of cardstock or thick paper cut into the following dimensions (at least one of each size strip per student):
  - 1" x 6"
  - 1" x 10"

- Plastic drinking straws (3 per student)
- Scissors
- Various kinds of tape (duct, scotch, masking)
- Safety goggles
- Stopwatch

STEAM Exploration Steps

1. Before the lesson, arrange the materials into organized and labeled trays.
2. Read aloud the picture book *The Girl Who Thought in Pictures* or share biographic information about Temple Grandin. Here are some main ideas you may want to include:
    □   Temple Grandin is an innovator in animal behavior and has designed several products to help animals. (She's a leading designer in humane slaughter facilities.)
    □   She is twice-exceptional, meaning she has a special need (autism), but is also a very curious and gifted innovator.
    □   Speaking out for children and adults with autism is a passion of Grandin. Her childhood was not always an easy one; she was often misunderstood and had a difficult time in some of her schools. She was sent to a special school on a farm later in her childhood. Working with the animals and teachers at that farm changed her life. At 18 she designed her first invention, a "hug box" for those with autism.
    □   Grandin's love for learning started long before her first invention. She was a curious child. She loved to design and redesign bird kites to make them fly. One of her first wonderings was if her bird kite would fly higher if she bent its wings. She learned that it did! This only made her more curious. (This is the hook for today's exploration.)

3. Share the STEAM challenge with your young innovators (see Appendix: STEAM Challenge Cards). Tell students that they are little engineers for the day and will help young Temple explore to create a flying toy.
4. Read aloud *Rocket Science for Babies*. (Teachers of older children, don't be thrown off by the title; this book easily explains through diagrams the concepts of gravity, lift, thrust, and drag—the four forces that will act on their airplanes as they fly through the air.) If you don't have a copy of this book or another age-appropriate aerospace book for kids, ensure that children begin to understand or are curious about the following topics:
    □   *Gravity* is the force pulling down on all of us, all of the time. This is what will pull the airplane you create down to the ground.
    □   *Lift* is what is lifting the plane into the air. In this case, the loops or circles on the plane are lifting the plane into the air and helping to keep it there.
    □   *Thrust* is what propels the plane. In this case, it's you pushing the plane forward to fly!

□ *Drag* is also thought of as air resistance. It always moves in the opposite direction of the object in motion. If you move your hand rapidly side to side you can feel that air resistance.

5. Share a model airplane that you've created in advance (see Figure 20). Ask your students to analyze the design to see the part-to-whole relationship of how the items are used to create the plane.

6. Test the model flying toy you created to let students determine how it flies best, with the small end in the front or the large end in the front. Students will notice that the toy flies better with the small end in the front.

7. In the challenge, Grandin asks for students to create *the best* flying toy. Ask students: *What does it mean to have the best toy?* Work together to brainstorm a list of characteristics that may describe a well-designed flying toy. The following list includes sample characteristics that students may consider the best. You may ask them to connect to what they already know about airplanes to help them determine these characteristics.
    □ Height (how high the toy flies)
    □ Distance (how far the toy travels)
    □ Durability (how well the toy holds up to multiple tests)

8. Let students "window shop" the materials you have gathered. You can choose to limit the number of materials each child uses, or not. For younger children, or children who need visual directions, you may want to create a visual poster with photographs of the directions (similar to the playdough directions from Chapter 3). If you are working with very young children, or children with significant motor delays who may not be ready yet to build a plane independently, you can create this toy in a small group using a hand-over-hand technique. Or you can create several models of the different types of airplanes for students to explore with and collect data on. Students can still let an "I wonder" question guide them as they select the plane they want to test. Do what best works for the needs and readiness levels of your students.

9. Draw students' attention back to the flying toy characteristic lists (created in step 7) and materials. Tell them that they will create their own wondering question to guide their exploration. Ask students to think back to the STEAM challenge to see if anyone can remember Temple's wondering. (She wondered if her bird kite would fly higher if she bent its wings.)

10. Have students partner talk using the *I Noticed, I Wonder* journal. Students will use the materials, the diagram of the flying toy you've created, and the characteristics to write (or verbalize) their wondering. Some sample statements include the following:

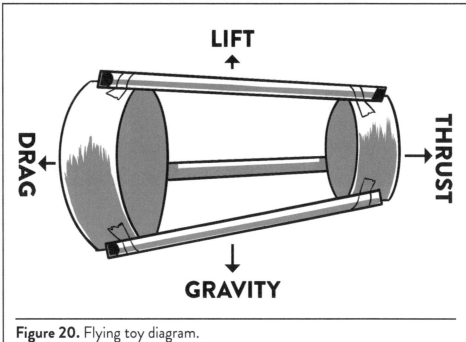

Figure 20. Flying toy diagram.

> □ I noticed that we can use up to three straws. I wonder if three straws will make the toy fly longer before crashing.
> □ I noticed that we have two size options for paper. I wonder if the toy will fly higher if I use two smaller strips rather than one of each size.
> □ I noticed that we have scissors. I wonder if my toy will fly farther if I cut my straw in half and make a shorter flying machine.

Ask students to record these wonderings either on the journal page or a class anchor chart.

11. Set your young engineers free to explore and create. Although students are creating their own flying toys, they should still be talking and sharing thoughts with others while they work. Examples of aircraft created by students can be found in Figure 21.

12. Designate a test area in your classroom or hallway, or, if the weather is nice, you may want to take your engineers outside. Here are some important ideas to note as they test, share, and reflect:
    > □ Students will need to select at least one of the criteria from your characteristics chart to collect data for (e.g., height, distance, durability). You may choose to record the data on a chart with the whole class or have students do so independently or in partners. Students with a higher level of readiness may choose to record data on more than one characteristic.
    > □ Students will perform multiple tests using their aircraft.
    > □ Students will need to collect data based on how their toy flies.
    > □ After a few tests, students will likely notice something that they want to adapt about their design (e.g., more tape, a different size loop). This is great—let them! Children are synthesizing information to determine what may work better.

Figure 21. Flying toy examples.

- ☐ Listen for engineering vocabulary words for content and thinking (e.g., *height*, *distance*, *gravity*, *lift*, *thrust*, *drag*) as students discuss and create their designs.

13. Once students have tested their designs, ask them to share their flying toy with the rest of the class. Ask if they think they have created "the best" flying toy for young Temple. Remind them to use their data to help express why or why not their toy was the best.

14. **Exploration extension ideas.** There are many variations you can test. Add more straws, add more loops or different sizes of loops, test outside or inside, or cut the straws to different sizes. Students' wonderings are the limit. Measuring speed is an additional challenge that some students may be interested in exploring (Speed = Distance/Time).

Innovation Process Summary

The primary innovation strategy featured in this lesson is wondering. The STEAM challenge shares young Temple's wondering about how to create a better bird kite. Children use that wondering as a model to help them write a wondering statement that will guide the creation and design of a flying toy. As with previous lessons, wondering is not the only strategy used in this lesson. Children will naturally move through most, if not all, of the strategies that encourage innovation and creativity. Other strategies that may be useful to point out in this lesson include connecting and growth mindset.

Connecting. In this lesson student build schema by thinking through what they know makes a flying machine like a plane work well.

Growth mindset. As students are testing their design, they will most likely find things that don't work as well as they would like. They will ask to change materials, add more tape, take off an extra loop, etc. These modifications should be encouraged. Learning to see mistakes, synthesize that information into new learning, and adapt their design indicates a high level of thinking for little learners.

CHAPTER 6

DEEPER UNDERSTANDING:
MAKING INFERENCES

Encouraging deeper thinking in young children involves teaching them to make inferences. Inferring, or drawing conclusions based on reasoning, can be a challenging skill for students of all ages, but especially for our youngest learners who are still actively building schema. Very young children make inferences by taking clues from the environment. Logical reasoning was previously believed to begin around the ages of 4–5. However, recent research (Clark, 2015) points to what many early childhood educators and families already suspected: Babies are capable of logical reasoning and deductive reasoning even before they are 1 year old.

When inferential thinking is posed in a way that meets the interest and readiness levels of young learners, it will pique students' curiosity. Inferring is an important thinking skill in STEAM investigations because students are constantly wondering and problem solving as they tinker and explore. They need reasoning skills to be able to brainstorm hypotheses and draw conclusions from observations. This type of deeper thinking requires students to reason by:

- making observations as they explore,
- connecting to what they know about those observations (schema), and
- drawing conclusions or making inferences based on those two pieces of data.

How Do Teachers Help Students Make Inferences?

When introducing inference to young learners, show examples using nonverbal communication as an engaging starting point. In my classroom, students would begin by working in partners. One person would act out an emotion, and then he would draw or write about that emotion. His partner would have to identify the emotion and tell or circle the clues that helped her draw that conclusion (e.g., I knew you were happy because you were smiling, laughing, and dancing; I knew you were nervous because you were shaking and biting your fingernails). This activity is great because it not only incorporates writing and reading, but also connects to a young learner's schema. The ability to read nonverbal cues is one of the early inferences that young children will learn to make, so this is an activity they can more easily relate to.

Like the previous thinking strategies, encouraging deeper thinking begins with the environment. Your classroom and lessons should be filled with books that inspire inferences or share examples of inferential thinking, like *Now and Ben*, the book featured in this chapter's STEAM lesson. For materials, you will want to use items that encourage curiosity or problem solving. Materials that require students to explore how objects work will require reasoning and inference. Examples might include determining how to build ramps for cars in a block center and building a marble run from LEGO bricks. Listen to your students' words. Phrases like "Maybe if . . ." or "So that must mean . . ." are like gold to young learners and educators. They are the clues that let you know a student is making inferences. Teaching students to use these sentence stems and listen for their classmates saying these words can help them realize when they are making inferences. The following are a few ideas of things you can do to encourage making inferences in innovative and creative thinking.

- **Create an environment that requires students to be curious and problem solve organically.** Setting up materials and explorations in inquiry-inspired learning kits (like those used in the STEAM exploration in this chapter) will require students to make inferences even as they figure out how to explore. Also, surround students with books that either require them to make inferences (i.e., infer how a character feels based on pictures or text clues) or share examples of innovators making inferences (e.g., *Now and Ben*, the book featured in this lesson).
- **Teach children this common thinking routine for making inferences:**
  - Explore → Notice → Connect → Infer

- **Use thinking stems.** Help students notice when they may be making inferences, or teach them the language to share inferences by using thinking stems like the following:
  - ☐ I noticed . . . and I think if . . .
  - ☐ So this must mean . . .
  - ☐ Maybe if . . .

Journaling and Anchor Charts: Making Inferences

The following can be used as anchor charts or as journal pages to record thinking as students learn to make inferences and use this strategy to explore the concept of innovation.

- *So This Must Mean*: This chart draws on children's senses and emotions to help them make observations, share what they notice, and make inferences as they write or draw what they think their observation may mean.
- *Collecting Clues*: This journal or anchor chart asks students to collect clues by recording observations, connect to schema by sharing what they know about a topic, and then record inferences. (This tool is modeled in the sample inferences lesson in this chapter.)
- *Sketch, Maybe if*: Students sketch what they noticed during an experiment or exploration on this organizer and then make a plan and a prediction for what they think may be the next outcome or step.
- *Inference Notes*: This journal page or anchor chart works as a place for individual students or the whole class to collect "Maybe if . . ." or "I think . . ." thoughts as they explore together. Similarly to the *Growing My Mind* organizer (see Chapter 3), it provides a great opportunity for students to see how their inferences and deeper thinking take place over the course of a unit of study.

So This Must Mean . . .

	Sketch what you notice.	Write what you think this means.
See		
Hear		
Touch		
Feel		

Collecting Clues

What I noticed. ➡ **What I know about that.** ➡ **What I infer.**

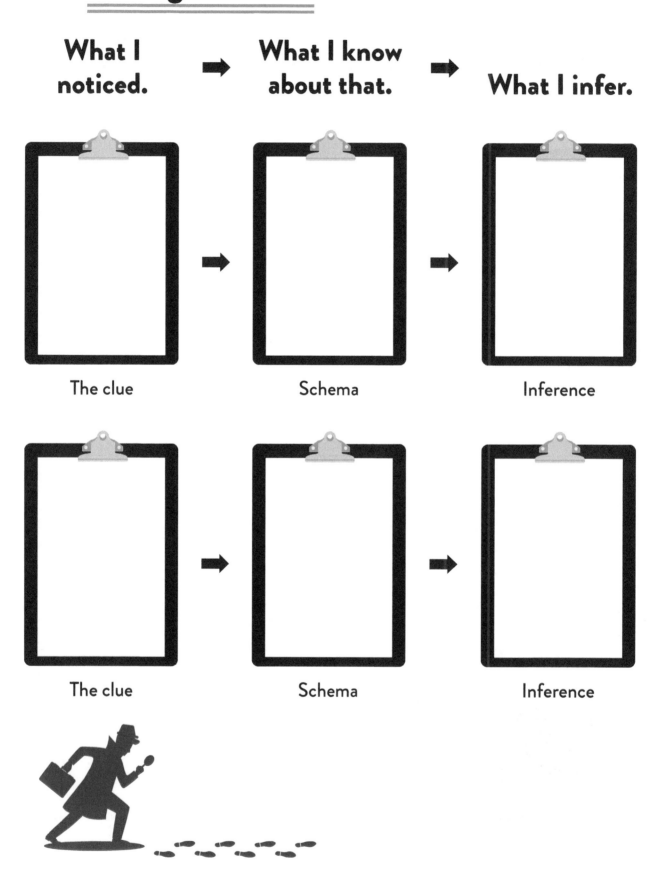

The clue   Schema   Inference

The clue   Schema   Inference

Sketch

Draw a sketch or diagram to share what you noticed.

Maybe if . . .

What do you think might be a good next step? Write a plan for what you will try next.

Inference Notes

"Maybe if . . ."

"I notice . . . I think . . ."

STEAM Exploration

Animal Adaptation Innovation

The student journal pages and anchor charts shared previously in this chapter can be used in many different learning experiences and content areas to help students understand how to develop deeper understandings as they make inferences. As an additional resource, this model STEAM exploration will give students an opportunity to explore inference even further.

Introduction

Benjamin Franklin is known as a founding father of the United States of America, but he was also a very successful innovator. From the time Ben was a very young boy, he was exceptionally curious, often getting into trouble with his parents. Both of Ben's brothers died in water-related accidents, so his father forbade him from being in the water. However, Ben was determined to find a way to swim safely and helps others do so as well. When he was 11 years old, he noticed that ducks could swim for hours without tiring. This observation led him to infer that if people had webbed feet, they could also be safer in the water. He invented two wooden swimming fits that are similar to the plastic flippers that divers use today (see Figure 22). This invention is the hook for making inferences in this chapter's STEAM exploration. Students will explore various types of animal adaptations in five different stations and then create their own innovation inspired by an animal adaptation, just like Benjamin Franklin did with the flippers.

In this STEAM exploration:
1. Students will read or listen to *Now and Ben*, a picture book about Benjamin Franklin that shares examples of his inventions and what we use today that is comparable.
2. Students will read or listen to the book *What Would You Do With a Tail Like This?* After reading the book, the teacher and students will model the *Collecting Clues* inference journal page by creating an anchor chart and adding examples from the text.
3. Students will explore five stations to learn about various animal adaptations. The stations themselves are set up with materials but no written directions. As a class or in small groups, students will look at the materials and determine the best way to explore with the materials in each kit.
4. Students will choose an animal adaptation, either from their exploration stations or from an animal they already know, and design an innovation based on that adaptation that could solve a problem. Students will use the *Collecting Clues* journal page to help them brainstorm their animal adaptation and innovation.
5. Students will create a prototype or model of the animal adaptation innovation in a loose parts lab.

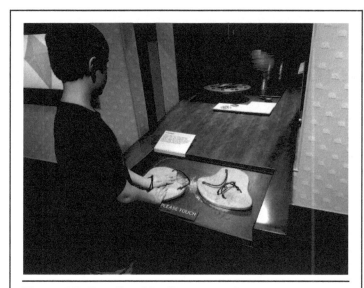

Figure 22. Ben Franklin flippers replica.

Innovation Focus

Inference

Featured Innovator

Benjamin Franklin

STEAM Challenge

Young Benjamin Franklin is a curious boy. He wonders about everything, especially everything that *really* interests him, like swimming. Young Ben hates getting tired when he swims. He notices that ducks have webbed feet to push them along in the water, and they can swim for hours. Ben creates wooden duck-like flippers for himself to help him swim. Although they don't work perfectly because they are a little heavy on his feet, the idea that he can create animal-inspired inventions to help solve problems sets his mind on fire. Now his mind is full of too many wonders to test alone. He needs an engineer like you to help him think, create, and design! What do you say, young innovator? Are you up for the challenge?

Vocabulary

Animal adaptations, infer

STEAM Exploration Materials

- Student journal page: *Collecting Clues*
- Book: *What Would You Do With a Tail Like This?* by Steve Jenkins and Robin Page
- Animal adaptation (structural adaptation) station kits:
  - Ears: construction paper rolled into paper cones
  - Blubber: lard in a resealable plastic bag, bowl of ice water, gloves
  - Beaks: chopsticks, tweezers, tongs, spoon, beans, sunflower seeds, rice, gummy worms, plastic insects
  - Claws: child-sized glove with a plastic spoon hot glued on each finger to look like claws, tray of dirt
  - Webbed feet: 3 craft sticks duct-taped to look like webbed feet, 3 craft sticks taped without a web, container of water

- Loose parts*: clay, toothpicks, feathers, craft sticks, scissors, construction paper, and small rocks

* You can use any recycled item or material for loose parts that you have readily available in your classroom.

STEAM Exploration Steps

1. Read aloud the book *What Would You Do With a Tail Like This?*
   - Draw a three-column chart on the board similar to the journal page *Collecting Clues* (with columns for the Clue, Schema, and Inference).
   - Tell students that, in order to help young Ben think about how animals can help solve problems, they will need to look for clues.
   - Begin filling out the anchor chart with clues from the book. See Figure 23 for an example.
   - As you read, complete the clues organizer as a class using two of the animals in the book. See Figure 24 for an adaptation chart used in a preschool classroom.

The Clue (What I Noticed)	Schema (What I Know About That)	Inference (What I Infer)
I notice that rabbits have large ears that move independently.	I know rabbits being able to move their ears independently helps them listen.	I infer that this keeps the rabbit safe from predators.

Figure 23. Example anchor chart for collecting clues.

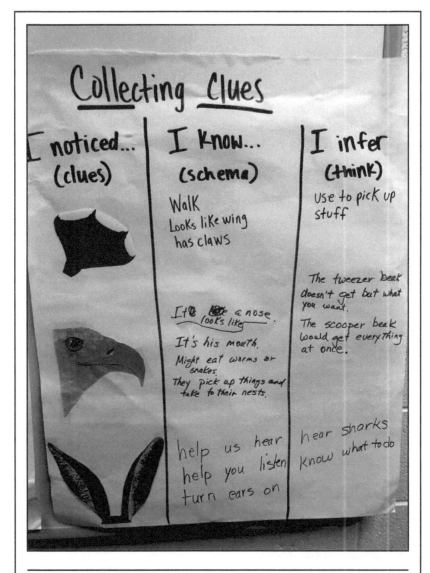

Figure 24. Preschool adaptation anchor chart.

2. Young Ben asked students to help him think about how these animals' body parts (or adaptations) might be the clues we need to help solve a human problem. Ask students to discuss the following in pairs: *Take a look at our "Collecting Clues" chart. How could these animals' body parts (or adaptations) help solve a human problem?* Answers will vary (e.g., rabbit ears on a teacher might help her better hear her students on the playground; elephant ears on a person may help him stay cooler by allowing him to fan himself).

3. Distribute animal adaptation kits for students to explore. If you want students to explore with every kit, you can have students rotate through them like centers. Alternatively, you can have students explore with one or two kits of their choosing and then share their findings with the class using the *Collecting Clues* journal page. No one way is right or wrong; do what works best for your students.

4. Review the materials of each kit with students. The items should be arranged in containers or tubs (see Figure 25). You will notice that there are no written directions for these kits. Tell students: *Because today's focus is making inferences, we will begin by inferring how to explore with each kit. For example, I notice that the webbed feet kit has two types of feet and water. How might we explore to learn from this kit?* Students can then test each type of foot in water.

5. As students explore, ask them to discuss these questions:
   □ *What animals does this exploration remind you of?* A student may say that the lard in the zipper bag reminds her of whale's blubber. This question requires students to connect to schema and what they know about animals.
   □ *How does this body part (or adaptation) help that animal?* The student may say that the blubber keeps the whale warm in the cold ocean water. This question helps the student think and make inferences about how this feature protects the animal.
   □ *How could this feature (or adaptation) help humans?* The student may say that coats made of blubber could help warm people who work outside in winter. This question helps the child make inferences about how this feature could help humans.

6. Add a few more rows to the *Collecting Clues* anchor chart that the class created together earlier. As students share what they learned in the investigation, add their thoughts to the anchor chart.

7. Ask students to think about the animal features they studied today (or adaptations they knew from previous experiences) and choose a favorite. Then, have them think about what human problem that body feature would solve.

8. Distribute a blank sheet of paper to each student. Have them write or draw the problem they would like to solve and the animal feature that will help them solve the problem (e.g., When people work outside in the winter, it is very cold. I want to design a coat with blubber pockets to keep people warmer). See Figure 26 for student examples.

Figure 25. Animal adoption kits.

9. Give each group a loose parts lab tray or set up a loose parts station for the whole class to use. Challenge your students to build a model of their animal adaptation that will be used by a person, or a model of a person using the animal adaptation to solve the problem (e.g., a model of a blubber coat or a model of a person wearing a blubber coat).

10. When students finish and have cleaned their area, display their 3-D artwork and their problem in the classroom or another location where others can see it.

11. As a reflection, ask students to share what they learned about animal adaptations and what they wonder now.

Innovation Process Summary

The primary innovation strategy featured in this lesson is making inferences. The STEAM challenge shares the real-world example of young Benjamin Franklin exploring with creating webbed feet to help him swim better. In order to do this, he had to take what he knew about webbed feet helping animals and make the inference that this adaptation would work to solve his problem. This exploration asks students to follow that same process. Other strategies that may be useful to point out in this lesson include connecting and wonder.

Connecting. In this lesson, students build schema as a part of the process of making inferences. Students are required to tell what they know about the animals to help them think about what might be true (the inference).

Wonder. Curiosity, or wondering about ways to solve different problems, is a key component to this exploration. Students are asked to wonder about animals' body features or adaptations and how they may help solve problems that humans face.

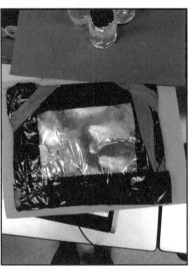

Figure 26. Animal adaptation samples.

REFLECTION

The ability to reflect is a critical skill in innovation. Play-based learning experiences and STEAM explorations should include reflection. The art of reflection is closely tied to all of the other innovation strategies shared in this book. Reflection encourages students to engage in metacognition, or thinking about their thinking, with each of these innovation strategies. Reflection is the glue that holds this entire process together. The purpose for engaging students in STEAM explorations is to encourage deeper thinking in young children and also to help them practice these important lifelong thinking routines. How does a baseball player learn to run faster? How does a hockey player learn to hit a slapshot? She does so with repetitive practice, specific feedback, and trying again a little differently based on what she's learned. The same is true for innovative thinking. A student hones his innovative and creative thinking by practicing the skill, reflecting on what was learned, and then using that skill again. Meaningful reflection is what makes the cycle of lifelong learning possible; through this metacognitive strategy, all other thinking routines are refined.

How Do Teachers Foster Reflection?

Reflection is most commonly thought of as occurring at the end of the lesson, but through the use of the strategies listed in this book, students can reflect throughout the learning cycle as they play and explore. As with making inferences, students' language is often a good indicator to determine if they are reflecting. You may hear them speaking in the past tense in the middle of the investigation (e.g., "I thought. . . ."). This is a good indicator that students are reflecting. Teaching children to use the thinking stem "At first I thought . . . but now I think" is a good way to encourage reflection while still keeping the focus on moving forward. In early childhood, emotional responses are also a sign of reflection. If you see an emotional response, like a student laying her head on the table in the middle of an investigation, the child may be reflecting on something she tried that did not work. This would be a good time to respond with some growth mindset and mindfulness strategies.

Reflection, as it is used in this book, is the act of thinking about the experiment, but also thinking about the strategies used to explore. A common reflection used at the end of a lesson is having children think about what they have learned and what they wonder now. As children think about their own thought processes through opportunities like this, they begin to grow as independent innovative and creative thinkers. Although there are several journal pages to encourage reflection in this section, it is also important to note that almost any of the journals from the previous chapters can be used for reflection, because reflection encompasses all of the innovation strategies. The following are a few ideas of things you can do to encourage reflection in innovative and creative thinking.

- **Reflect throughout.** Encourage students to reflect not only at the end of a lesson, but also throughout the exploration as they problem solve. Model think alouds with reflection as you work with students during the investigation.
- **Teach children the importance of reflecting as a step to lifelong learning.** This can be taught by connecting the types of reflection done in sports or other topics of interest to the students you teach. Reflection is a lifelong skill, so it can be found in every career or enjoyable activity that may interest children.
- **Share with an authentic audience.** Give children opportunities to share authentically with adults and peers about not only what they learned, but also their thinking process and what they determine to be the most important aspects of their investigation. This will encourage meaningful reflection.

Journaling and Anchor Charts: Reflection

The following can be used as anchor charts or as student journal pages to record thinking as students explore this strategy and learn to reflect and think metacognitively.

- *At First I Thought, Now I Think*: This tool will allow students to jot down or draw what they believed at the beginning of a unit or an investigation. Then, at the end of the investigation, students will draw or write about how their ideas have changed based on new learning. (This is the tool modeled in this chapter's STEAM exploration.)
- *The Most Important Thing*: Students will use this organizer to determine the most important topics as they reflect on an exploration or topic of study. Teachers can also use this as an anchor chart to record what students feel was the most important learning that occurred in an exploration or unit of study.
- *All of the Things I Explored!*: This journal allows students the opportunity to think about all of the explorations or observations they investigated during a unit of study. This could be used as a culminative anchor chart or journal page to help students reflect on a variety of learning experiences provided throughout a unit of study. This will work as a great tool for those using UDL because it will clearly show multiple representations and student choice in learning.
- *Sketch, Wonder*: This journal provides an opportunity for students to reflect at the end of an experiment or exploration. Students will sketch what happened, draw or write about what they wonder now, and then describe how they will test this wondering in another experiment. This is a great extension or challenge for young learners.
- *Here's What Happened*: In this journal, students will draw or write about the outcome of their investigation. Then, they will write or draw about what they hope to explore next.

At First I Thought . . .

Draw or write what you thought when you began the project.

Now I Think . . .

Sometimes innovators change their minds as they learn. Draw or write about how your thinking changed as you explored.

The Most Important Thing

Draw or write about the most important thing you want others to know about your work.

All of the Things I Explored!

Draw or write about all of the things you learned as you explored.

Sketch

You've worked hard. Sketch a picture or diagram to describe what happened in your exploration.

Wonder

What do you wonder now?

How would you test this wondering?

Here's What Happened

Draw or write the outcome of your investigation.

What will you explore next?

STEAM Exploration

Portable Planetarium

The student journal pages and anchor charts shared in this chapter can be used in many different learning experiences and content areas to help students understand how to reflect and think metacognitively about their current understandings. As an additional resource, this model STEAM exploration will give students an opportunity to reflect and investigate how ideas can change as they explore and learn.

Introduction

Neil deGrasse Tyson, an American astrophysicist, is the inspiration behind the final STEAM exploration in this book. When Tyson was 9 years old, he visited the Hayden Planetarium. This trip to see the stars inspired a lifelong love for learning about astronomy. He said, "so strong was that imprint [of the night sky] that I'm certain that I had no choice in the matter, that in fact, the universe called me" (as cited in Brodeur, 2014). When he was a teen he began gaining some notoriety in the field by giving lectures on astronomy. Tyson is now the director of the same planetarium that first piqued his curiosity of the cosmos.

The STEAM exploration for reflection asks children to help young Neil design and create a portable planetarium to view the stars when he cannot get to the Hayden Planetarium. Students will take a look at star patterns in the night sky, learn the myths behind constellations, and design their own constellation for a portable planetarium using black paper and a flashlight. As students finish, they will share their creations and stories, and reflect on what they thought at the beginning of the investigation and what they think now that they have completed the exploration. In this STEAM exploration:

1. Students will build schema and connections to planetariums and the night sky by using either a book about constellations or an app that shows the patterns of stars in the sky.
2. Students will plan, design, and create their own star pattern or constellation.
3. Students will explore the meaning of the words *transparent*, *translucent*, and *opaque* as they create their portable planetarium.
4. Students will reflect and share using the organizer *At First I Thought, Now I Think*.

Innovation Focus

Reflection

Featured Innovator

Neil deGrasse Tyson

STEAM Challenge

Our dear friend Neil needs your help! He's just visited the planetarium and is absolutely in love with studying the night sky. He saw a show about how the stars move across the sky and noticed that there were patterns not only in how the stars move across the sky, but also in how the stars are grouped together. These special groups of stars are called constellations. He's packed his telescope and walked outside only to be greeted by a cloudy sky and pouring rain. Neil has an incredible idea: Let's bring the night sky inside, just like they do at the planetarium! What do you say, young astronomer? Will you help bring the outdoors in by designing and creating your own illuminating portable planetarium?

Vocabulary

Constellation, light, opaque, translucent, transparent

STEAM Exploration Materials

- Student journal page: *At First I Thought, Now I Think*
- Various books, videos, or apps about the night sky, including constellations
- Portable planetarium materials:
  - ▢ Flashlights or pop lights (one per student)
  - ▢ Black poster board or tag board cut to the size of the lens on the flash light or pop light (one circle per student)
  - ▢ Hole punches (one per table or group of students)
  - ▢ Foam board, golf tee, and child-safe mallet (per table or group; for punching holes that the hole punch cannot reach)
  - ▢ White, silver, or yellow crayons
  - ▢ A piece of clear plastic (or transparent material) and colored plastic (or translucent material)

STEAM Exploration Steps

1. Have students take a look at the night sky. Due to the fact that you see your students during daylight, you may want to assign this as a family engagement activity. You may also want to look at the night sky together in a simulated environment, like on your computer, using VR goggles, or on an app on your phone (see Step 3 for more info).

2. Here are some interesting things you may want to be sure your students observe. Remember to get them to observe by asking what they notice and wonder:
    □   Notice how the moon changes in a pattern (stages of the moon).
    □   Notice how the stars move across the sky over time.
    □   Is the night sky moving, or are we moving? (The Earth is moving; it just looks like the sky is moving.)

3. Introduce the concept of constellations to students by sharing a constellation and the story behind it. The book *Zoo in the Night Sky* by Jacqueline Mitton is great to leave in your reading center for children to explore, but there are many other wonderful books about constellations available at your local library. Don't shy away from a book about the stars because you think it looks too challenging. Children can learn a lot from the pictures alone. Night Sky is a free app available on most phones that is phenomenal for sharing the night sky, constellations included. There are several other free or low-cost apps that are similar. By pointing the phone or tablet in the direction of the sky, you can see where that constellation will appear at night.

4. Tell students that they will now plan their own constellation. Have them brainstorm an animal or person they wish were a constellation. Give them a sheet of blank paper and crayons or star stickers, and let them plan their constellations.

5. The constellation has been created; now it's time to use students' imagination. Have students do a quick write (or quick draw) to share the story behind their newly created constellation.

6. Distribute night sky paper (pieces of poster board or tag board cut to the size of the lens of the flash light or pop light). Have students use pencils or light-colored crayons to transfer their constellation plan onto the night sky (see Figure 27).

7. Using either a hole punch or a golf tee and a soft mallet (depending on the age of your students and size of your night sky), ask children to put holes in their paper where they want the stars to be.

8. Have students tape their night sky papers onto their flashlight or pop light.

9. Your young astronomers are now ready to share! Turn off the overhead lights and let students take turns sharing their constellation and their story (see Figure 28).

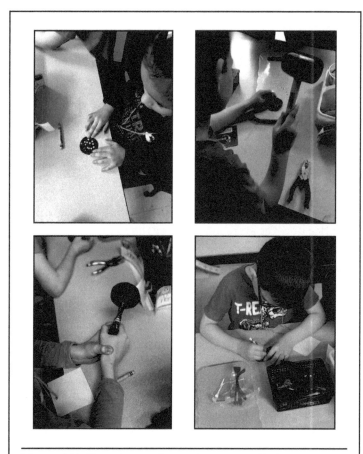

Figure 27. Planning and creating constellations.

10. After students have shared, be sure to talk about light and how their mini-planetariums work. Ask questions like the following to guide your discussion:

  □ How are we able to see our stars? (The light shines through the paper.)

  □ Why does the light shine through some parts and not others? (The holes allow the light to pass through.)

  □ Is there anything we could put over the light that would still allow the light to shine through? (Test a transparent material like clear plastic.)

  □ Why does the light not shine through the night sky paper without the holes? (The paper is opaque.)

  □ Is there anything we could put over the holes that would allow some of the light to shine through, but not all of it? (Anything translucent—scarves or colored plastic party bags made from cellophane, for example—will work to let students explore opaque, translucent, and transparent materials and how the light passes through each differently.)

11. Either create an anchor chart as a class as a group writing experience or distribute the corresponding student journal page *At First I Thought, Now I Think.* This metacognitive reflection requires students to think about how their thinking has changed and process more deeply. An example of an answer might be: "At first I thought that stars were just spread out across the sky each night. Now I understand that they are grouped in the same patterns each night, like constellations."

Figure 28. Portable planetarium example.

Innovation Process Summary

The primary innovation strategy featured in this lesson is reflection. The STEAM challenge shares a hook asking children to help young Neil design a planetarium he can shine in his bedroom. After the children explore and create, they are asked to reflect on what they first thought and what they think at the end of the lesson. The reflection journal modeled in this lesson, *At First I Thought, Now I Think*, helps students understand how their thinking can and should change during an investigation as they learn and develop new ideas. Other strategies that may be useful to point out in this lesson include empathy and inference.

Empathy. In this investigation, students are helping their friend Neil. They are working to understand why he loves space and helping him through the frustration of wanting to look at the sky during the rain by creating a planetarium.

Inference. Students make inferences as they explore how their handheld planetarium works (e.g., I see that the light is not shining through the whole flashlight anymore, so I'm inferring that this is because the black poster board is opaque).

REFERENCES

Bailey, B. A. (2000). *I love you rituals*. New York, NY: HarperCollins.

Bemiss, A. (2018). *Hands-on STEAM explorations for young learners: Problem-based investigations for preschool to second grade*. Waco, TX: Prufrock Press.

Bloom, B. (Ed.). (1956). *Taxonomy of educational objectives: The classification of educational goals. Handbook I: Cognitive domain*. New York, NY: Longmans Green.

Brodeur, N. (2014). Neil deGrasse Tyson: 'I still jump into puddles in the rain.' *The Seattle Times*. Retrieved from https://www.seattletimes.com/seattle-news/neil-degrasse-tyson-lsquoi-still-jump-into-puddles-in-the-rainrsquo

Casap, J. (2019). *What problem do you want to solve? Asking the key questions through Austin and Boston!* [Video file]. Retrieved from https://www.youtube.com/watch?v=_iDRZDktx7o

CAST. (2018). *The UDL guidelines*. Retrieved from http://udlguidelines.cast.org

Catmull, E., & Wallace, A. (2014). *Creativity, Inc: Overcoming the unseen forces that stand in the way of true inspiration*. New York, NY: Random House.

Clark, C. (2015). Babies have logical reasoning before age one: Deductive problem solving was previously thought to be beyond the reach of infants. *Emory Health Sciences*. Retrieved from https://www.sciencedaily.com/releases/2015/11/151118131813.htm

Conscious Discipline. (2019). *Living room: Kindness ritual*. Retrieved from https://consciousdiscipline.com/free-resources/shuberts-home/living-room/kindness-ritual

Dweck, C. S. (2006). *Mindset: The new psychology of success*. New York, NY: Random House.

Dweck, C. (2015). Carol Dweck revisits the 'growth mindset.' *Education Week*. Retrieved from https://www.edweek.org/ew/articles/2015/09/23/carol-dweck-revisits-the-growth-mindset.html

Harvey, S., & Goudvis, A. (2007). *Strategies that work: Teaching comprehension for understanding and engagement* (2nd ed.). Portland, ME: Stenhouse.

Maslow, A. H. (1943). A theory of human motivation. *Psychological Review, 50,* 370–396.

News.com.au. (2013). *Littlewoods retailer survey finds mothers asked 228 questions a day*. Retrieved from https://www.news.com.au/lifestyle/parenting/little-woods-retailer-survey-finds-mothers-asked-228-questions-a-day/news-story/9cca3e25f5981147d1e0bff293f6e3f2

Peterson, R. (1992). *Life in a crowded place: Making a learning community*. Portsmouth, NH: Heinemann.

Project GEMS. (2011). *Innovation model*. Retrieved from https://www.wku.edu/gifted/project_gems/innovation_model.php

Ricci, M. C. (2017). *Mindsets in the classroom: Building a growth mindset learning community* (Updated ed.). Waco, TX: Prufrock Press.

Roberts, J. L., & Inman, T. F. (2015). *Strategies for differentiating instruction: Best practices for the classroom* (3rd ed.). Waco, TX: Prufrock Press.

Sheffield, L. J. (2003). *Extending the challenge in mathematics: Developing mathematical promise in K–8 students*. Thousand Oaks, CA: Corwin.

Stanford d.school. (n.d.). *A virtual crash course in design thinking*. Retrieved from https://dschool.stanford.edu/resources-collections/a-virtual-crash-course-in-design-thinking

Wagner, T. (2012). *Creating innovators: The making of young people who will change the world*. New York, NY: Simon & Schuster.

Yong, E. (2018). What we learn from 50 years of kids drawing scientists. *The Atlantic*. Retrieved from https://www.theatlantic.com/science/archive/2018/03/what-we-learn-from-50-years-of-asking-children-to-draw-scientists/556025

STEAM
CHALLENGE CARDS

Creative Coding Space Race

STEAM Challenge: Katherine Johnson has loved math since she was a very little girl, maybe even younger than you. Now she works for NASA as a human computer! Working alongside her dear friends Dorothy Vaughan (a computer programmer) and Mary Jackson (an engineer), she is solving a challenging problem to help bring an astronaut home safely from space. Are you ready to hear the most exciting part? She has asked for help from a team of young engineers like you! So, what do you say? Are you ready to help solve this coding challenge to bring the astronaut home safely?

Creative Chemistry Lab

STEAM Challenge: Chocolate chip cookies, Silly Putty, Slinky, sticky notes, Play-Doh, Band-Aids—did you know that these things were all invented by accident? It's true! Noah McVicker was working in his family's soap company when he accidentally invented Play-Doh. Silly Putty was created by accident, too. Now it's marketed as a toy, but did you know that it has been used by astronauts in space to hold their tools down in zero gravity? Young innovators, you are challenged to recreate playdough in our Creative Chemistry Lab. Then, you will put on your creative thinking caps and create a new use for this accidental invention, just like astronauts discovered that Silly Putty could hold objects in space!

It Matters to Me: Makerspace

STEAM Challenge: You are never too young to be a world changer! Anna Stork and Andrea Sreshta were in college when they noticed that people needed help after a devastating earthquake. They wanted to help bring light to those in need, so with a simple solar panel, a plastic bag, and a sports bottle cap, they invented a light to help people see when there is no electricity after a natural disaster. Easton LaChappelle wanted to help people who couldn't use their hands. He was only 14 when he designed a robotic hand using LEGO bricks! What do Anna, Andrea, and Easton have in common? They each had a problem they wanted to solve and the heart to help. Now, they have a challenge for you. What problem do you want to solve? Put on your innovator eyes and your hardworking hands, because today you will have the chance to create your own innovation to solve a problem that is heavy on your heart.

Wonder Workshop: Flying Toys

STEAM Challenge: Young Temple loves to create and fly her bird kites out of old scraps of paper. Last week she wondered if a kite would fly differently if she folded the wings. After some fun exploring and playing outside, she learned that it did—the kite flew higher with bent wings! Now, she can't stop wondering if there are other ways to make toys that fly. She wanted to make a new bird kite but doesn't have any paper large enough. All she can find are some strips of paper and plastic straws. Temple wonders if it's possible to turn that trash into flying treasure. What do you say, young engineer? Will you explore to help Temple design the best flying toy possible?

Animal Adaptation Innovation

STEAM Challenge: Young Benjamin Franklin is a curious boy. He wonders about everything, especially everything that really interests him, like swimming. Young Ben hates getting tired when he swims. He notices that ducks have webbed feet to push them along in the water, and they can swim for hours. Ben creates wooden duck-like flippers for himself to help him swim. Although they don't work perfectly because they are a little heavy on his feet, the idea that he can create animal-inspired inventions to help solve problems sets his mind on fire. Now his mind is full of too many wonders to test alone. He needs an engineer like you to help him think, create, and design! What do you say, young innovator? Are you up for the challenge?

Portable Planetarium

STEAM Challenge: Our dear friend Neil needs your help! He's just visited the planetarium and is absolutely in love with studying the night sky. He saw a show about how the stars move across the sky and noticed that there were patterns not only in how the stars move across the sky, but also in how the stars are grouped together. These special groups of stars are called constellations. He's packed his telescope and walked outside only to be greeted by a cloudy sky and pouring rain. Neil has an incredible idea: Let's bring the night sky inside, just like they do at the planetarium! What do you say, young astronomer? Will you help bring the outdoors in by designing and creating your own illuminating portable planetarium?

ABOUT THE AUTHOR

Allison Bemiss was born into the education world. She spent her childhood years tagging along with her mother to hands-on mathematics and science workshops, playing with pattern blocks and building (and destroying) bridges alongside leading educators, long before STEAM became an educational buzzword. Allison has worked to encourage creative innovative thinking in early childhood and elementary-age children for 15 years, while serving as a teacher, interventionist, and education consultant. She currently works for the Green River Regional Educational Cooperative developing workshops for early childhood and elementary educators. When she is not hard at work developing the next STEAM exploration, you can find her at home with her two exceptionally curious sons, history-loving husband, energetic dog, and know-it-all cat. She is an advocate for twice-exceptional education, special education, early childhood education, and play-based learning throughout childhood. Allison is thrilled to hear from students and teachers. Connect with her on Twitter @teacherallison.

STANDARDS ADDRESSED IN THIS BOOK

Common Core State Standards for Mathematical Practice

1. Make sense of problems and persevere in solving them
2. Reason abstractly and quantitatively
3. Construct viable arguments and critique the reasoning of others
4. Model with mathematics
5. Use appropriate tools strategically
6. Attend to precision
7. Look for and make use of structure
8. Look for and express regularity in repeated reasoning

Common Core English Language Arts Standards: Speaking and Listening Grades K–3

Comprehension and Collaboration:
- CCSS.ELA-LITERACY.SL. (K.1, 1.1, and 2.1) Participate in collaborative conversations with diverse partners about (grade level) topics and texts with peers and adults in small and larger groups.

- CCSS.ELA-LITERACY.SL.3.1 Engage effectively in a range of collaborative discussions (one-on-one, in groups, and teacher-led) with diverse partners on grade 3 topics and texts, building on others' ideas and expressing their own clearly.

Next Generation Science Standards: K–3 Engineering Design

Students who demonstrate understanding can:
- K-2 ETS 1-1 Ask questions, make observations, and gather information about a situation people want to change to define a simple problem that can be solved through a new or improved object or tool.
- K-2 ETS 1-2 Develop a simple sketch, drawing, or physical model to illustrate how the shape of an object helps it function as needed to help solve a given problem.
- 3-5 ETS 1-1 Define a simple design problem that can be solved through the development of an object, tool, process, or system and includes several criteria for success and constraints on materials, time or cost.
- 3-5 ETS 1-2 Generate and compare multiple possible solutions to a problem based on how well each is likely to meet the criteria and constraints of the problem.
- 3-5 ETS 1-3 Plan and conduct an investigation collaboratively to produce data to serve as the basis for evidence, using fair tests in which variables are controlled and the number of trails considered.